Seeking Truth Together:

Enabling the Poor

and Saving the Planet

in the Manner of Friends

Horizon Society Publications
45 Bellevue Drive
Boulder CO 80302
After November 1, 2000:
4475 Sioux Drive, Apt. 001
Boulder CO 80303
Published in 2000

Library of Congress Cataloging-in-Publication Data

Powelson, John P., 1920-
      Seeking Truth Together: Enabling the Poor and Saving
          the Planet in the Manner of Friends

     1.   Church and Social Problems—United States
     2.   Church and Social Problems—Society of Friends
     3.   Society of Friends and world politics
     4.   Society of Friends—Doctrines

    ISBN 0-9618242-2-0

Table of Contents

Preface

"Seeking truth together" lies between Unity and Disagreement. It is a new way for Friends to discuss socio-political issues. We do not seek Unity on all social issues, for then we would be inadequately diversified as a Society. Nor do we attempt to persuade each other of our own viewpoints.

Instead, "seeking truth together" calls on Friends to meet in small discussion groups (here called "workshops") on social, political, or economic topics; to collect all relevant facts on each topic (and to agree on which facts are relevant); and to listen carefully to the viewpoints of all Friends present, some of which may come from logic and some from Divine leading. To understand better, it would be well for Friends who disagree with some viewpoint to repeat it before answering it. (To save space, these repetitions are not made in this book). Without the craving to persuade of one's own stand, Friends may calmly discuss alternatives, meditate on proposed policies, and seek Divine assistance. It is suggested that a tiny silence (say, two seconds) be observed between speakers, to make sure that none is cut off. The meeting might be closed with a longer period of silence. Friends would leave with their views, possibly changed, but at least seasoned in the manner of Friends.

How do Friends make an impact on the world? Is it by all of us agreeing on some position - such as opposition to war - and making our weight felt? Or is it by being a Society of Seekers, who listen to each other in Friendly fashion, learning to voice the individual and collective opinions of sincere, concerned people?

It is, of course, by both ways. But this little Quakerback suggests that because the second way is so light, it possesses greater weight. This book is intended to show, by example, how to seek truth together in the Society of Friends.

I would be happy to start a dialogue with Friends and other readers. Those with comments are invited to send them to me by email at jack.powelson@colorado.edu or by regular mail.

Jack Powelson	After November 1, 2000:
45 Bellevue Drive	4875 Sioux Drive Apt. 001
Boulder CO 80302	Boulder CO 80303

Language

In a laudable effort to make the English language gender-neutral, it has been customary to write "he or she" instead of the universal masculine, and to use the plural, "their," with singular subjects. This satisfies the needs of feminists, but it aggravates the needs of authors like me, who wish to be grammatical and non-verbose.

In order to satisfy both needs, I have used 'one' to indicate "he or she" or "his or her" and 'one's' instead of "their." To indicate when "one" or "one's" is used in this new sense, as opposed to the old one, I have placed it in single quotation marks. If the world adopts my suggestion, the single quotes will no longer be needed, since context will indicate which meaning is intended.

Acknowledgments

I am greatly indebted to my wife, Robin Powelson, and to Jane Kashnig of Milwaukee Meeting, for reading the manuscript and making suggestions. Jane especially read every chapter thoroughly and often turned it upside down with her original ideas. J.D. von Pischke went over the entire manuscript and made many grammatical corrections, in addition to substantive suggestions. Gusten Lutter of Mountain View Meeting (Denver) and Jerry Van Sickle also offered valuable comments.

I am also indebted to the Earhart Foundation for financial assistance in meeting the costs of this publication.

Chapter 1

This Book Does Not Answer the Questions it Raises

Presumably, Friends seek Truth together. We gather in business meeting to consider a given question whose truth may not be the answer that any one Friend thought at the outset. In our thoughtful deliberations, we listen carefully to each other and construct a *corporate* position called Unity, or Sense of the Meeting. We do not *persuade* each other of the righteousness of our own position, but we seek the corporate position together.

We do, don't we? Well, maybe. Maybe sometimes. Anyway, that is the ideal.

I have often tried - without success - to *persuade* Friends of my positions on social and economic issues. I have traveled under concern to many Quaker gatherings in the United States, Australia, and New Zealand - Meetings for Worship, Yearly Meetings, and twice to Friends General Conference. My wife, Robin, would always accompany me.

My first Quakerback, *Facing Social Revolution,* explains the social issues I encountered around the world. My second Quakerback, *Dialogue with Friends,* laments that Friends did not always see my Light.

My "road to Damascus" occurred at Friends General Conference in 1999, where I conducted a workshop of twenty participants, which was intended to last for five sessions. I started out on Monday by explaining the thesis of my most recent book, *The Moral Economy.* Immediately, objections arose, and the objectors spoke loud and long, so much so that I could not express my views adequately. By the end of the third session, ten participants had walked out and formed their own workshop. For one who has always been rated highly as a teacher, and whose books have always had positive reviews, I was stunned. Never had anything like that happened to me, nor would I have expected it among Friends. My eyes brimmed with tears, and I had to get a grip on myself to continue the workshop with the remaining ten.

I reported the disaster to Jane Kashnig, clerk of the workshop committee. Jane had read my Quakerback, *Facing Social Revolution,* and was generally sympathetic with my classic liberal outlook. "Those Friends could have left your workshop on Monday," she said, "but even though they were uncomfortable, they stayed because they were willing to consider difficult, real world issues. Your ideas are sound and deserve serious consideration by Friends."

"But I am about to present my topic at workshops in four Yearly Meetings. How can I prevent the same thing from happening?"

Jane thought for a moment. Then she said, "Did you *tell* the workshop your truth, or did you seek the truth *with* them?"

"But Jane," I replied, "I have studied history for thirty years, and economics longer than that. I *know* that much that they were saying was false."

"It may have been objectively false," Jane replied, "but it was *their truth*, and you have to respect it. Furthermore, even in a statement that is mostly false, there is often *some truth*. That's what you should be looking for."

So this third Quakerback, *Seeking Truth Together,* tries to be more within the ideal of Friends. Each chapter represents a "workshop," or gathering of Friends, whose purpose is not to persuade the reader of *my* position or any position, but to seek the corporate Light. Some of the meetings were called workshops, others interest groups, still others just meetings or discussions. For simplicity, in this book I have called them all workshops.

After all sides of a subject are presented - my own and others - each workshop tries to allow the Truth to find us. Instead of writing the book I had once intended, I now present a dialogue between workshop participants and myself.

I have several goals in mind:
1. To supply adequate, unbiased, and true information on each subject.
2. While presenting my own opinions, to strive to seek the Truth together with other participants rather than to persuade them of my truths.

3. To write a book on how to conduct a discussion on these and other difficult issues in the manner of Friends.

The workshops faced a problem common to Friends' Meetings. We greet each other at Meeting, talk about how we love each other and we all want peace, but if there is an issue on which we disagree, we stop talking about it as if it no longer exists. Many Friends do not share my classic liberal outlook, so they don't talk with me about political issues at all. I once showed an article I had written for *Friends Journal* to a member of my Meeting who I knew disagreed with my philosophy. I asked her if she could help me make my ideas more understandable to Friends who shared her outlook. She replied that she and I saw the world so differently that there was no point in talking about it.

If Meetings are distilled down to the issues on which we all agree, such as the weather, then we have a poor basis for a religion. To counter that, this book takes up *hard* issues, that are not normally the subject of Friends' discussions. Or if they are, it is assumed that all Friends take the same position on them, when in fact some of us don't. I have often felt alienated in my own Meeting because it is just assumed that everyone feels the way I don't on a given issue.

After my "road to Damascus," instead of explaining the thesis of *The Moral Economy* I placed the book on a table, pointed to it, and said to the workshop participants, "I have just written this book. Now, let's pretend I had not written it, and you tell me what to put in it. What do you perceive as wrong, or immoral, about the present world economy?"

Chapters 3-18 of this Quakerback take up the Wrongs that Friends mentioned, not just in 1999 but in all my travels. Each chapter heading is a statement made by Friends. Not all Friends agreed with these statements, and mostly I myself did not. But each statement was the truth to the Friend who uttered it, and our task was to seek the Truth together. Chapter 19 asks whether a Quaker or an economist can better touch the hearts and minds of people. Chapter 20 questions whether there is such a thing as spiritual reform, as opposed to political or economic. Chapter 21, by Jane Kashnig, explains how she found the Quaker religion to be holy ground for seeking Truth.

To be clear about my own economic philosophy, I have asked Gusten Lutter - who has read all my books on these subjects - to explain in Chapter 2 "where the author is coming from." In Chapter 3 and thereafter we will seek to know where other Friends are coming from, and whether we can seek Unity together.

Chapter 2

Classic Liberalism and Classic Quakerism:
Where the Author is Coming From

by Gusten Lutter

Jack Powelson has spent thirty years studying the development of the liberal economy and has found that a *classic* liberal economy - i.e., in the original concept of liberalism - is accompanied by increased freedom and respect for the individual, as well as greater opportunity for all. He has also found that the classic liberal economy increases contact between people in all walks of life, and that with that increased contact comes greater trust and a larger sense of community and belonging. As a Quaker, he believes that this liberal economy embodies one of the basic Quaker tenets: that there is that of God in everyone, and thus that everyone should enjoy freedom of conscience in religion, and choice elsewhere.

In his studies he found that efforts to force people to do or be good seem to backfire or fail, that very often these efforts are accompanied by oppression and injustice, and usually are performed without consulting the people that are meant to be helped. Not only that, but he saw that the power to do good can become a vested interest and actually interfere with real improvements in people's lives. In his studies he also saw many examples of moral actions that were brought about, not by government but by a growing social conscience in individuals, and which now are willingly performed within the context of the liberal economy. He wrote *The Moral Economy* to describe ways in which a liberal economy could address the difficulties his Quaker compassion sees in the world: oppression, pollution, poverty, ignorance, disabilities. Based on his studies, he believes that a market system can more efficiently and more creatively deal with these problems than any system that tries to legislate, regulate or force them out of existence.

5

Here is a whimsical summary of thirty years in Jack Powelson's research life:

Principle #1: The Quaker ideal of freedom of religious conscience should be extended into as many areas of life as possible.

> *Surprising discovery 1a:* Everything works better when individuals are in charge of their own lives.
>
> *Surprising discovery 1b:* Despite the effort required, people are generally happier when they make choices.
>
> *Surprising discovery 1c:* It's amazing how well people choose when they choose for themselves. (And how badly when they choose for others).
>
> *Surprising discovery 1d:* It's amazing how quickly people learn to make good choices when they suffer the consequences of bad choices.

Observation #1-1: While it may be morally right to act in someone else's best interest, it's much more effective when you ask him or her what that interest might be.

> *Surprising discovery 1-1a:* It's amazing how seldom the do-er consults the do-ee.
>
> *Surprising discovery paraphrased:* Rarely are the peasants asked what they want.

Observation #1-2: It is frightening to take responsibility in one's life in an area where one has not exercised it before.

> *Surprising discovery 1-2:* People will demand more benefits from their caretakers (government) than they are willing to pay for.

Principle #2: Trust comes from (will come only from) working together, not from guarantees outside the relationship.

> *Surprising discovery 2a:* Compromise is good.
>
> *Surprising discovery 2b:* Trade is a relationship.

Principle #3: If I can do good to you (not *for* you), then I can do you harm as well.

> *Surprising discovery 3a:* People who might happily do something on their own out of compassion resent and resist doing that very thing when forced to.

> *Surprising discovery 3b:* In order to retain the satisfaction which I get from doing good, I will prevent you from taking control of your life, so I can continue to do good to you.

> *Surprising discovery 3c:* Power bestowed by office is subject to the whims of the officeholder. The officeholder's *personal* willingness to do good is a precarious basis for mutual trust.

Principle #4: Power expands until other power stops it.

> *Surprising discovery 4a:* The exercise of power to force people to do things is not only oppressive, it is inefficient and counterproductive.

> *Big surprise 4b:* Which brings us right back to Principle #1 and Surprise 1a!

Chapter 3

"The Rich are Getting Richer and the Poor are Getting Poorer."

Once my workshops had voiced their near unanimous belief that the rich are getting richer and the poor poorer, I would ask: "How long has this been going on?" Usually the answer was, "Since the dawn of capitalism."

"Let's look at the evidence," I would suggest. Archeological findings for the Maya show that poorer people were shorter and died earlier than the rich. Virtually all early societies held slaves. Historical records of literate societies - ancient Greeks, Romans, Egyptians, and Chinese - support the proposition of a far more uneven distribution of wealth than is present in the West and Japan today. In England in the seventeenth and eighteenth centuries, scholars concluded that nobility, gentry, and rentiers earned about fourteen hundred times the incomes of soldiers and laborers. By studying the tax and financial records of cities in medieval Italy, historians have reported enormous gaps between rich and poor, far greater than the multiple of 326 that today separates CEOs of major corporations from ordinary workers.[1]

If all that is true, the distribution of income has become *more* egalitarian, not less, since the dawn of capitalism. Participants in the workshops were surprised, but they accepted the historical record. What caused incomes and wealth to become more evenly distributed?

Here's a hint: The change took place only in northwestern Europe and Japan, primarily after the Industrial Revolution of the eighteenth century. It did not happen in the rest of Asia, or in Africa, or in Latin America, or in eastern and southern Europe; indeed, in these less developed areas, the distribution of income and wealth is far more skewed today than it is in the industrialized world. We will discuss those countries in Chapter 8.

The change occurred *as a result of capitalism*, not in spite of it. (Participants were surprised, but they listened attentively). As

8

machinery became increasingly employed, the productivity of labor went up, because a worker with a machine can produce more than one without. How would the increment be divided between the capitalist (owner of the machine) and the worker? That would depend on the relative scarcity of each. If capital (money to buy machines) was in short supply, a high return would have to be paid to persuade its owner to invest it in some risky innovation. So more of the increment would go to the capitalist. If workers were scarce relative to machines, capitalists would bid workers away from other capitalists by paying higher wages, so more would go to the worker. In nineteenth-century United States, workers were scarce relative to capital, so workers could demand a large part of the increment. From at least mid-century to the end, wages rose, while the return on capital remained fairly stable at about 3% throughout the century. In mid-nineteenth century, workers were receiving about 50% of gross national product, by the end of the century close to 70%.

From about 1970 on, however, the traditional narrowing reversed itself, and the gap between rich and poor started to widen. So, the participants were right after all, but only for recent years. Why? By operation of the same economic laws. Now, however, the technological revolution causes a greater demand than supply of trained technicians, such as electronic engineers, physicists, and other scientists. Companies bid them away from each other by offering higher wages. Inventors, also scarce, reap high profits if successful. On the other hand, an over-supply of less-skilled workers keeps their wages depressed.

Add to that the stock market. As prosperity grows in the United States, investors believe that profits of companies will continue to increase. So they bid up stock prices. Traditionally, the value of a stock depends on the earnings of the company. Many stocks trade at five or ten times the company's earnings per share, but in recent years the price-earnings (P-E) ratio of technological companies has been advancing rapidly. Microsoft stock currently trades at about 60 times earnings. Some say that because of new computer technology, old norms (P-E ratios) no longer apply, and higher ratios will be permanent. Thus the 46% of American families who own stocks have become much richer, at least on paper, than those who don't.

Another reason for the gap is that high-income workers tend to marry each other, as do low-income workers as well. Suppose two workers earning $200,000 marry each other. Their average household income increases from $200,000 to $400,000, though no real change has occurred. Suppose two other workers earning $20,000 also marry each other, so their family income average rises to $40,000. The gap in average family incomes between the rich pair and the poor pair also doubles, from $180,000 to $360,000.

In the real world, the increase in two-income families, along with increasing wages all around, widens the gap. *The Economist* argues that the change in family structure is among the most important reasons for the widening gap, after the disparity in technical knowledge and the stock market.[2] A still other reason, albeit minor in quantity, is the increase in immigrants and single-parent families, who tend to fall at the lower end of the scale.

Economists are not agreed on whether the incomes of the poor are decreasing absolutely or just relative to the newly-rich. Unfortunately, economic statistics do not tell us, because they are not a science. We speak of real income as income adjusted for price changes (e.g., how much the wage of an hour of labor will buy in consumer goods). If, however, we use one price index we may show real income as declining while a different index shows it rising.[3] All economists agree that the gap has been widening, but they disagree on whether the poorest brackets are holding their own in terms of purchasing power, or declining.

My guess is that they are holding their own, or even rising slightly. I base this not on income data but on the houses they own, television sets, automobiles, and other consumer goods that they buy. Also, the labor cost index compiled by the Federal Reserve - which shows the total cost of labor including all benefits - has been rising steadily. Another study by the Federal Reserve finds that the average wealth of every type of household, including ethnic minorities, increased from 1983 to 1989, except for one: single women with children.[4]

Finally, beginning in the mid-1990s the wages of the poor seem to have increased because of an increased demand for unskilled labor, but the gap is again widening because the salaries of the professionals are increasing even more.[5] The Federal Reserve has shown an increase in the net-worth gap between rich and poor families from 1997 to 2000. Some economists point out, however, that the rich-poor gap always increases in a dynamic society, since those who promote innovations gain while others lag behind. Only later on do the laggards catch up. For example, the states in the United States where innovations are greatest are those where the income gap has grown most of all.[6]

Despite general prosperity, there remains an underclass that seems not to lift itself. Actually, the underclass changes its composition, some rising out of it and others falling into it. I do not deal with that in this chapter, but in Chapter 12 on welfare.

"What shall we do about it?" I asked my workshops. Some favored offering tax breaks and benefits to low-end workers. A few suggested a socialist government, but most - aware of the disaster of the Soviet Union and other socialist countries - rejected that idea. Some favored a redistribution of incomes, through a negative income tax (if your income is high, you pay the tax; if it is low, you receive a "tax"). Indeed, I propose this in *The Moral Economy,* but I suggest that the redistribution be only great enough to keep the poor in food and housing but not enough to dissuade them from working.

I do not concern myself much with wealth gained from the stock market. Stocks rise and fall, and there are indications that those who gained from investments may be heading for a fall. Many of the symptoms of the years preceding 1929 are being repeated today. In the 1920s investors were saying that new technology (radios, automobiles, improved machinery) was creating a *sustainable* higher normal level of P-E ratios, just as is being said today about computers. I myself am not sanguine on the stock price bubble lasting, but other economists disagree.

Finally, the laws of supply and demand are very difficult to beat. So the most constructive way of closing the gap is to convert low-skilled workers into high-skilled. This is happening, with greater enrollments in professional and technical schools. But it is very, very slow.

The historical truths persuaded the participants in my workshops, and they could not think of any dramatic action to narrow the gap further. Neither could I. So, after a moment of silence, we moved to the next topic.

NOTES

[1] I have assembled information on distribution of income and wealth in earlier societies in *The Moral Economy,* page 41, and at various points in *Centuries of Economic Endeavor* and *The Story of Land.*

[2] *The Economist,* 11/5/94.

[3] This is explained in *The Moral Economy,* pages 52-54.

[4] *Wall Street Journal,* 6/19/95.

[5] According to a study by two Washington think tanks, the Economic Policy Institute and the Center on Budget and Policy Priorities, "Pulling Apart: A State-by-State Analysis of Income Trends," reported in *The Wall Street Journal,* 1/18/00 and The *New York Times,* 1/19/00.

[6] *New York Times,* 1/24/00.

Chapter 4

"Affirmative Action is Being Reversed"

Is affirmative action intended to open businesses and schools to more minorities, or is its purpose to change the hearts and minds of those who discriminate against them? Does forcing affirmative action on employers who resist it cause them later to accept it, or does it stiffen their resistance? My workshops, which almost unanimously favored the affirmative action laws, mostly sounded as if they had not heard of this question.

They all recognized, as I do, that racism continues in America. For example, "in interviews [of employees of American Eagle, a commuter carrier for American Airlines] . . . current and former employees say that racial slurs were as common as tire changes inside the hangar . . . In an era when blue-collar jokes and biting ethnic humor are as close as shock-jock radio, some white mechanics never imagined that their black co-workers might take offense."[1]

I am a strong proponent of affirmative action. Robin and I did not send our children to all-white schools; I do not want to have all-white colleagues in my work. Yet I believe that affirmative action should spring from the hearts and minds of people, who implement it in their lives because it is right, not because the law demands it. Therefore, I say that affirmative action laws should be repealed. But other Friends pointed out the successes of these laws.

First, affirmative action laws have created opportunities for minorities that they would not otherwise have enjoyed. Oliver Lee, "son of an illiterate garbage man with a third-grade education . . . , was plucked from an all-Black junior high in Savannah, GA, in 1965 to attend Cheshire Academy, a Connecticut prep school."[2] Later he became a successful lawyer. Davidson and Grofman list many such cases in *Quiet Revolution in the South*.[3] An exhaustive study by the former presidents of Princeton and Harvard shows that minority students admitted to elite universities have fared much better after graduation than a control group of minority students equally eligible for admission but turned down for lack of space.[4]

Second, affirmative action laws *have* changed the hearts and minds of some. When I taught for one semester in a small college in Georgia, one colleague told me he had been brought up to believe Blacks were inferior people, but his association with black students after integration had changed his mind. Virtually all my white students said the same. When I asked the one black student in my class whether she felt at ease with her white counterparts, she said Yes (but every time I saw her socializing, it was with other black students).

I affirmed the positions of these other Friends. So, if we were to re-run history, I am not sure if I would favor affirmative action laws or not (I did when they were passed). But past is past. I do believe they should be repealed now, for five reasons:

First, they have divided our society and caused many lawsuits. One of my white students in Georgia resented her turn-down from a more prestigious university. She argued that Blacks with qualifications inferior to hers had been accepted. White students have sued universities,[5] as well as Boston Latin School, for the same reason.

Second, the Equal Employment Opportunity Commission (EEOC), while performing some valuable service, has gone way beyond its mandate by demanding that businesses hire employees not suited for their jobs. I will mention some examples in the following section.

Third, our country is moving toward voluntary acceptance of affirmative action. University administrations increasingly agree that students are better educated in a diverse environment. Selection criteria should not be based on academic merit alone, but on providing each student, of whatever origin, the opportunity to meet and discuss with students of different backgrounds.

Fourth, as businesses globalize, their management sees advantages in hiring high-level staff of diversified origin. If you want to buy or sell in Africa, it helps to have an African for a manager.

Fifth - and this is my strongest reason - if the institutions of society - family, church, and schools - believe laws relieve them of their responsibilities to be personally or collectively involved in promoting social justice, they may not inculcate in their children the willingness to accept people of different origins. I was saddened that Friends in my workshops advocated laws to enforce affirmative action more than they supported First-Day school classes to teach the insidiousness of racism.

While Government action to favor special groups has many positive effects, some adverse consequences must be recognized, including cases where affirmative action has instilled hatred. In the next section, I include not only the affirmative action laws but also the Americans with Disabilities Act. In the section after that I will cite examples of how the public increasingly accepts voluntary affirmative action and rules to welcome those with disabilities into the wider society.

Adverse Consequences

1. Duke Power Company had a policy of not promoting employees unless they were high-school graduates or could pass a written test. The Supreme Court ruled against that policy, on grounds that it froze the status quo of discriminatory practices. Duke argued that the policy promoted efficiency. I believe the benefit of the doubt should have gone to the employer, but not all in my workshops agreed.
2. Exxon had a longstanding policy of not hiring employees with drug addictions. Ruling that addicts were a disabled group protected by the Americans with Disabilities Act, the EEOC demanded that Exxon hire them.[6]
3. "In 1992 a Federal court ruled that the District of Columbia must hire a fireman who was HIV-positive because there was 'no measurable risk' that he could transmit the disease in the line of duty - despite the fact that he might be required to perform mouth-to-mouth resuscitation to fire victims."[7]
4. "A worker fired from Radio Shack for stealing claimed he was disabled by post-traumatic stress syndrome caused by a previous robbery of the store and therefore was protected under the

Americans with Disabilities Act. Radio Shack paid him off rather than spend $30,000 fighting the case."[8]

5. Suit was filed against United Parcel challenging its policy that drivers should have sight in both eyes. Another suit was filed against Aloha Islandair for refusing to hire a pilot with only one eye.[9] In still another case, one court found that "a truck driver who sees out of only one eye but whose brain had compensated for the deficiency was disabled and therefore entitled to sue the employer who had dismissed him."[10]

6. Fifty black parents shouted down a white teacher, Ruth Sherman, because she used the book *Nappy Hair* in her classroom. She tried to explain that the book taught a young black girl, previously ashamed of her kinky hair, to be proud of it. The parents would not listen, and Ms. Sherman's relationship with them was so damaged that she transferred to a different school. While this incident does not stem directly from affirmative action laws, I wonder whether these laws did not help create the underlying divisiveness. Somehow, I am reminded of the Quaker story, *Thee Hannah,* which has a more gracious ending. (Has thee read it?)

7. The mayor of Washington, DC, was forced to accept the resignation of an official who had used the word "niggardly." In fact, "niggardly" is derived from Scandinavian languages and has no racial overtones.[11] Once again, no direct relationship to affirmative action laws, but maybe an indirect one.

8. Many cases have been documented of minority-owned businesses that receive preference for government contracts even though they are not low bidders, who have subcontracted with white-owned businesses at a slightly higher price, dividing the difference (paid by taxpayers) between them.[12]

9. "Many black and Hispanic owners of large businesses are arguing that the traditional definition of a minority-owned company - a company in which members of a minority group own 51% - limits their ability to raise capital by selling stock." If they respond to the opportunity to increase their size and sales, but only non-minority investors have the capital to invest, they would lose their preferred status by growing.[13]

10. "According to CNN, in 1985 a group of black investors that included [OJ] Simpson and [Colin] Powell bought a television station in Buffalo, NY, and benefited from a federal minority preference program that gave them a tax break to buy the station. They sold it . . . at a healthy profit."[14]

Voluntary Affirmative Action

Friends agreed with me that affirmative action from the heart should be taught and practiced in all institutions of society. We do not know whether universities continue affirmative action because they were persuaded of its benefits while the laws were in force or whether they do so out of their hearts (or both). We do not know whether businesses practice voluntary affirmative action for competitive reasons or because it is right (or both). But I believe that in our wider society our hearts and minds are gradually changing, and businesses and universities follow the evolving norms.

1. When Proposition 209 became law, outlawing affirmative action in state universities, the University of California at Berkeley instituted a partnership with inner-city schools, intended to bring minority students up to the educational standards required for admission to Berkeley.[15] "Reeling from a series of reports showing decreased minority enrollment, the University of California has announced a plan to expand its college preparatory programs significantly, focusing on students who attend the state's worst high schools."[16] The program has been successful. "The number of black and Hispanic students offered admission to the University of California rebounded in the university's second year without affirmative action."[17]

2. In my own University of Colorado, our Department of Economics has been instructed to recruit minority professors.

3. "University of Michigan officials [report] that racial and ethnic minorities account for more than 25 percent of its 36,000 stu-

dents."[18] Possibly the affirmative action laws gave the impetus, but clearly the university wants to continue the practice.

4.   "Bans on affirmative action in Texas and California are producing efforts to develop alternative approaches that will maintain diversity in higher education without using race as a factor."[19]

5.   New York City's "school system agreed . . . to abandon race-based admissions and come up with a new enrollment plan that might increase consideration of students' economic hardships."[20]

6.   "Already in the United States, some firms are finding that cultural diversity leads to competitive advantage. 'They may be more attuned to an increasingly diversified population of customers. Equally, firms that continue to favour white men will find themselves fishing in a shrinking pool of potential employees.'"[21]

7.   "In the increasingly competitive environment of applying to elite colleges, the still small number of high-achieving African-American students are among the most coveted, wooed with free trips to campuses, personal attention from administrators and alumni, and a bevy of scholarships. The battles over affirmative action that have led many institutions to back away from giving preferences to minority applicants have intensified these recruiting efforts as colleges seek ways to keep their campuses racially mixed."[22]

Each of these propositions unleashed much discussion among workshop participants. We found unity that affirmative action should be practiced in all institutions of society. But we did not agree on whether it should be enforced by law. However, the purpose of the workshops was not to seek unity on all points. Instead, it was to open our minds to each other, to listen as well as to speak. We closed with a period of silence.

NOTES

[1] *Wall Street Journal,* 4/26/99.

[2] *Wall Street Journal,* 12/27/95.

[3] Davidson, Chandler; and Grofman, Bernard, *Quiet Revolution in the South: The Impact of the Voting Rights Act.* Princeton, NJ: Princeton University Press, 1994.

[4] Bowen, William, and Bok, Derek, *The Shape of the River: Long-Term Consequences of Considering Race in College and University Admissions,* 1998, reviewed in *New York Times,* 9/9/98; also *New York Times* editorial, 9/14/98. Some activists feared that this report proposed that civil rights had now won, when the big battle lies ahead; see *New York Times* editorial, 9/20/98.

[5] University of Texas: *Wall Street Journal,* 3/23/96, *The Economist,* 7/6/96; Boston Latin School, *The Economist,* 2/14/98.

[6] Bovard, James, *Lost Rights: TheDestruction of American Liberty,* New York, St. Martin's Press, 1994:171.

[7] Bovard *op. cit.,*:190.

[8] *The Economist,* 4/18/98.

[9] *Wall Street Journal,* 6/22/98.

[10] *New York Times* editorial, 4/26/99.

[11] *New York Times,* 1/29/99.

[12] *The Moral Economy,* page 78.

[13] *New York Times,* 10/12/99.

[14] *Wall Street Journal,* 10/8/95.

[15] *Wall Street Journal,* 1/6/97.

[16] *New York Times,* 5/23/97.

[17] *New York Times,* 4/4/99.

[18] *New York Times,* 5/10/99. See also *New York Times Magazine,* 5/2/99.

[19] *New York Times,* 4/23/97.

[20] *New York Times,* 2/18/99.

[21] *The Moral Economy,* page 76. The single quotes are from *The Economist,* 3/11/95.

[22] *New York Times,* 10/25/99.

Chapter 5

"We are Destroying Our Environment"

All participants in my workshops, myself included, agreed that human beings are damaging our environment. Ozone holes and global warming were tops in our concerns. Political institutions worldwide are not handling these concerns adequately. Treaty after treaty is broken. Why? If we all share this earth; if we all will suffer from the damage; if the means of correcting it are known - three "ifs" to which all participants agreed - why are we not stopping it?

The reason most participants cited is that we want our perks now, caring little for the future. We will cut down the forest now rather than save it for great grandchildren whom we have not met. Of course, "we" refers to everybody else, not the Friends in my workshops. Somehow, that explanation did not ring true to me. I do not believe people are so unintelligent or so little caring. There must be something more to it.

Here - I believe - is the "more:" We have gradually built a world economy of "free" resources, available for the taking, such as air, water, and forests. We pay for the purification and delivery of water, not the water itself. As we have sullied the air with bonfires, the winds have cleansed it. As we have dumped sewage into streams, the sun and wind have purified it. As we have buried trash, it has decomposed.

At some point in a growing world economy, however, a resource becomes "not free" - that is, polluted by overuse. At this point global warming and ozone holes set in. Also, water does not stretch to meet all needs. The wind cannot blow away all smog. The rivers cannot cleanse all sewage. But we have not known - or have disagreed about - the exact point where the earth can no longer sustain its abuse.

When a resource becomes no longer free, then someone must "own" it - that is, have the right to use it - and we do not know who. So polluters call upon their traditional "rights" to what has heretofore been free.

A certain amount of resources do remain free. The wind will clear away smoke up to a certain point. Running streams do cleanse themselves, up to a certain point. Do we take away the right to sully the air with bonfires, hitherto free, and hand it over to people who drive automobiles? The City of Pittsburgh, where I used to live, has done just that. In Boulder, my present city, we used to build fires in our fireplaces whenever we wanted; now we cannot do so on "pollution days."

So, who has the right to the diminishing percentage of resources that remain "free?" If ten per cent of a resource may be used without pollution, but ninety per cent is not "free," should all who use it pay an average of 90% of the cost? If so, how much and to whom? Or, should those who have used it "free" from time immemorial have grandfather rights to continue to do so? Or, should those who have never used it be allowed to catch up? These, writ large, are the questions that befuddle international negotiators.

They are no frivolous matter. Millions of dollars have been invested in developing a resource; more millions of jobs depend on it. Cleansing requires further investment. Who will pay for that? What about people in less developed countries (LDCs), who feel they have not had their proper share and cannot afford the cleansing equipment?

One solution, that I suggested to my workshops, was that environmentalists should buy the "right" to pollute from polluters and then retire it. I was using the analogy of the grocery store. Those who want bananas buy from those who have them. "Why should environmentalists pay," Friends retorted, "when they are acting on behalf of the rest of us?" I admitted I was kidding but was only emphasizing that *someone* has to pay. Why not those who want the results? If we do no more than forbid the pollution by law, the investors or jobholders pay - they are deprived of their use of hitherto free resources. Would it not seem fair that those who deprive them of their time-honored "rights" should reimburse them?

Instead of environmentalists, I suggested, the general public should buy the "rights" of the polluters. Friends in my workshops had a hard time with that. "Why should the general public pay," they asked, "to prevent polluters from doing wrong? We don't pay robbers not to steal, or murderers not to kill."

"No, we don't," I replied. "Civil societies have never condoned robbery or murder, but we have condoned pollution. Something that was previously right suddenly becomes wrong. Industries have always had as much legal right to pollute the air and water as we have to walk along streets or climb mountains. Suddenly, they are asked to sacrifice their livelihoods and their investments while the rest of us, who do 'beneficial' things such as teach in universities, get away scot free."

But that is not all. Some prominent scientists believe global warming and the threat to the ozone layer are either myth or not serious. They hold to the natural-cycles theory. The earth warms and cools in cycles lasting thousands of years. We have been measuring its temperature only in the past few decades, and we happen to have hit upon a cyclical downswing. Sallie Balliunas, an astrophysicist at the Harvard-Smithsonian Center, shows how the cycle of sun spots corresponds closely with that of the earth's warming. "The chairman of the Harvard-Smithsonian Center for Astrophysics asserts that the increase in greenhouse gases has been spread over the last century and most of the small earth temperature rises since 1880 had occurred before gases from human activity were being emitted." Richard Lindzen of MIT and Patrick Michaels of the University of Virginia find the global-warming models faulty.[1] A team of scientists headed by Howard Conway of the University of Washington in Seattle has just discovered that the melting of the West Antarctic Ice Sheet "may have been predetermined when the grounding line retreat was triggered in early Holocene time [up to 10,000 years ago]."[2] That study does not dispute that human activity may have aggravated the melting, however.

If we seek truth together, how is it that polluting industrialists are the very ones who adhere to the natural-cycles theory? The answer, I believe, is a human tendency toward selective perception - to "see" only the information that supports our pre-conceived viewpoint. I asked Friends in my workshops whether they also perceived selectively the information supporting theories of global warming and a widening ozone hole. Like the queries in our *Faith and Practice,* I did not insist on a reply.

One incident in my travels perturbed me greatly. At Pendle Hill, a Quaker study center, I was auditing a course on global issues. The instructor presented "proof" that the ozone hole widens because of human activity. Although I believe that too, I thought we should examine contrary evidence. One morning the *Philadelphia Inquirer* told of some scientists who argued that eruptions from Mount Pinatubo in the Philippines spewed forth far more ozone-destroying materials than human activity could unleash. I brought that paper to class and asked to read relevant parts. The instructor would not recognize me, saying that this material was not part of the course. I asked the twenty-odd students (only a few of whom were Quakers) if they agreed with that, and they did unanimously. Because I did not want to participate in a closed-thinking environment, I did not attend that course further. (Several years later, when half the participants in my workshop at Friends General Conference walked out - see Chapter 1 - I regretted that action. While at Pendle Hill, I should have stayed in the course and quietly participated as the way opened.)

Some Friends suggested that the International Organization for Standardization, located in Geneva, was the proper institution to set environmental standards through its ISO-1400 series, with which producers might comply in order to receive a stamp labeling them as environmentally-friendly. Those purchasing their products should be willing to pay a bit more to save the planet. I lauded their idealism, but my experience in many countries, where "anything" can be bought - drivers' licenses, right to vote - made me skeptical about widespread compliance. I felt that other pressures were needed to create environmentally-friendly producers.

What would these other pressures be? Here is a set of *general* principles by which producers might be induced to protect the environment. Once these principles had been followed for a period of time, the custom of following them would create new consciences, so that both producers and consumers would acquire the requisite morality.

First, all possible ways to reduce pollution should be explored. "In 1997, a group of two thousand scientists, including six Nobel laureates, found that 'there are many potential policies to reduce greenhouse-gas emissions for which the total benefits outweigh total costs,' with 'policies which are either inexpensive (such as encouraging consumers to buy energy-efficient appliances) or worth implementing whether or not global warming proves to be a problem (such as reducing subsidies to fossil fuels).'"[3]

Second, industries, farmers, and others throughout the world who have been polluting should be paid to stop. The bill will be huge. It should be paid by the whole world, according to means - therefore, the United States should pay the most. Instead of hugging trees, environmentalists might be looking for jobs for tree cutters whose work they would displace.

Third, pollution permits should be awarded for the amount of allowable pollution, on the basis of seniority (to those already polluting when restrictions go into effect). While the permits might be tradable, no pollution should be permitted for which a permit has not been issued. The Clean Air Act of 1967 and subsequent amendments might be a model. The basic principle is: "If you pollute, you pay the cost." Paying the cost to pollute would become just as acceptable (and moral) as paying for bananas in the grocery store.

Fourth, these are general principles only, but they should be the agreed basis for international negotiations, in which details would be worked out.

Many Friends held out for ISO standards and voluntary compliance. Other Friends needed time to think about my proposals or any proposals. Still others thought that with time they might think of better ways. In our closing silence we often found Unity on the problems - though a few Friends supported the natural-cycles theory - but not on the means of resolving them.

NOTES

[1] *The Moral Economy,* page 64.

[2] *New York Times,* 10/12/99.

[3] *The Moral Economy,* page 67. The section in single quotations is from *The Economist,* 6/14/97.

Chapter 6

"We Need a Higher Minimum Wage"

SCENE: A gathering of twenty Friends, for a discussion led by JP (the author of this book). For convenience, all other Friends are named OF (Other Friend), though each one speaking may be a different person. To save printing costs, the moments of silence after each speaker are not recorded.

OF: It is a disgrace to our society that so many workers struggle at subsistence wages, or even less. The minimum wage ought to be increased. (All except JP approved).

OF (turning to JP, disapprovingly): How can you be opposed, when you see the poverty around you?

JP: I too would like to see low-paid workers earning more, though I am not convinced a higher minimum wage will do it. Before turning to that question, let's consider who earns the minimum wage: mainly workers without skills, including teenagers – many black teenagers – and women just off welfare. In fact, almost all workers outside those categories earn higher wages.

OF: Then it should be increased just for those categories, shouldn't it?

JP: Let's hold off on that one until we examine some history. The first minimum wage law was passed in 1938, at 25 cents an hour, and the minimum has been going up every few years since then - almost yearly between 1961 and 1981. "At each point the unemployment rate for black teenagers tended to ratchet higher. By 1981, the unemployment rate for black teenage males averaged 40.7% - four times its early 1950 level . . . That year, the Federally-mandated Minimum Wage Study Commission concluded that each 10% rise in the minimum wage reduces teenage employment by between 1% and 3%."[1]

25

Increases in the minimum wage cause unemployment in the very groups it is intended to benefit. The law can force an employer to pay the minimum wage *if 'one' employs,* but it cannot force 'one' to employ.

Next, consider who really needs the minimum wage and who is getting it. "The first comprehensive study of the impact of the minimum wage, conducted by OECD [Organization for Economic Cooperation and Development] shows that the benefit of the minimum wage largely bypasses the poor, because relatively few low-paid workers live in low-income households, and relatively few low-income households have low-paid workers. In many poor households, no one is employed in a regular job. On the other hand, many low-income workers have well-paid partners or affluent parents. Since most low-paid workers are not in poor families, most of the income gains from the minimum wage would accrue to families that are not poor."[2]

OF: Yes, but how about workers who have been struggling on the minimum wage for years. Can't we do something for them?

JP: Actually, there is no permanent group of workers stuck at the minimum. Many who are at the bottom find that once they learn the ropes, they can work their way up. The most insidious effect of the minimum wage is that it prevents poor workers from being hired in the first place, and therefore they lose the opportunity to work up into higher positions.

OF: But how about family heads, with child dependents? Wouldn't they be better off with a higher minimum?

JP: There are a few of those. But "in fact, most minimum-wage work consists of part-time, non-career jobs in fast food, retailing or telemarketing, often filled by young, single, and middle-class workers."[3] The college kid needing a summer job often finds one at minimum wage.

Have you noticed, however, that gas stations are mainly self-service, and newspapers are frequently delivered by paid drivers in trucks? The kids that would have filled your tank or cleaned your windshield or delivered your papers have been priced out of the market by the minimum wage.

OF: But think of large, multinational corporations, where the CEO earns 326 times the wage of the lowest-paid worker. Wouldn't they be easily able to pay a higher minimum wage?

JP: Possibly, but large multinational corporations have very few workers at the minimum. In fact, they hire fewer workers overall, in proportion to output, than do small enterprises. Instead, the firms most affected are small ones, that hire 80% of American workers. Increases in the minimum wage have sometimes put small shops out of business, so workers have lost their jobs.

OF: Do economists other than you support increases in the minimum wage?

JP: Some do, but most do not. In October 1995 "more than 100 economists, including 3 Nobel laureates, . . . wrote in support of the proposed increase. A slew of recent empirical evidence seems to show that a moderate rise would not harm employment much, and one or two say it could raise it. But other economists disagree. Most . . . economists think that a 10% rise in the minimum wage would cut low-wage employment by 1-2%."[4] Virtually all economists say there will be some decrease in employment; the question is how much. "The September 1998 issue of the *Journal of Economic Literature,* an official publication of the American Economic Association, contains a survey of labor economists on the employment effects of the minimum wage. When asked to estimate the impact of raising the minimum wage, the average effect was estimated at minus 0.21%, meaning that a 10% rise in the minimum wage will reduce overall youth employment by 2.1%."[5] Are Friends content to have *some* persons forced into unemployment, no matter how small the number?

OF: Do any high-level government officials oppose increases in the minimum wage?

JP: Yes. Alan Greenspan, Federal Reserve Chairman, has said that "raising the minimum wage could deny some teen-agers their chance at entry-level jobs."[6]

OF: But won't an increase in the minimum wage help many workers and harm only a few, so we must consider the "greater good?"

JP: This is often said about war. Defeating the Serbs in 1999 contributed to the "common good," so President Clinton said a few "accidents of war" had to be countenanced, such as bombing civilians. Are Friends content to do harm to some persons for the "greater good?"

OF: Do we know specifically of any groups harmed by the minimum wage?

JP: Consider the following:

> Judge Sonya Sotomayor ordered a Manhattan business coalition to pay back wages to homeless workers who claimed they were being exploited as slave labor because they were being paid less than minimum wage. The defendants were Grand Central Partnership and the 34th Street Partnership, who were helping vagrants who used to hang around and sleep on area streets to develop the everyday coping skills necessary for holding down a job. The Partnerships would recommend them for permanent jobs with the local businesses that had been painstakingly persuaded to take a chance on the homeless. They had placed them in a social service program called Pathways to Employment, which provided temporary sanitation, security, office, and laundry jobs. That program is now virtually defunct, priced out of the market, thanks to Judge Sotomayor's ruling.[7]

I leave Friends with the following query: How many unemployed, unskilled workers are we willing to deny jobs in order to increase the minimum wage for other workers? How many small firms are we willing to drive out of business because they cannot afford the minimum wage? How would we explain to a job-seeking black teenager that we have diminished 'one's' probabilities, in order to promote the "greater good?"

Friends were perplexed. When one's long-held beliefs are challenged as they were today, one needs some time to think the matter over. Some said they needed to consult another economist. I encourage that. Whenever a controversial issue is raised in my class, I try to invite an economist who disagrees with me, so that all points of view can be expressed.

We closed with a disturbed moment of silence.

NOTE: This discussion did not occur in the fictional way indicated here. Rather, this chapter is composed of questions often asked me by Friends, and how I answer them. A few questions asked by my students at the university were also thrown in. The "disturbed moment of silence" reflects the high emotion that many Friends feel on this issue.

NOTES

[1] Bartlett, in *Wall Street Journal,* 5/27/99.
[2] *The Economist,* 6/27/98.
[3] Samuelson, in *Washington Post Weekly,* 4/29/96.
[4] *The Economist,* 4/27/96.
[5] Bartlett, in *Wall Street Journal,* 5/27/99.
[6] Associated Press news notice, in *Wall Street Journal,* 2/24/99.
[7] *Wall Street Journal editorial,* 6/8/98.

Chapter 7

"The Poor Need Affordable Housing"

SCENE: The same twenty Friends as in the preceding chapter.

After a moment of silence, JP opened with a question:

First Problem: Affordable Housing, Zoning, and Ghettoes

JP: With so much homelessness, and housing prices going up so rapidly, what shall Friends and others do about the many people who cannot afford a place to live?

OF: You know that I come from your home town, Boulder, Colorado. In Boulder, we have affordable housing, subsidized by the government, available only to low-income people. It's in a place called San Juan.

JP: Where in town is it located?

OF: I don't know, I've never seen it. I don't speak Spanish.

JP: I know where it is, but I've been there only once, to see a Chilean family our Meeting was sponsoring. They're good houses, but almost all the inhabitants are Hispanics. So, why do we isolate Hispanics in a ghetto? Why don't we instead give the dollar amount of the subsidy to low-income people, and let them find their housing where they will? Then they would be like the rest of us.

OF: Isn't it cheaper to build housing for the poor all in one place? Labor and transportation can be economized.

JP: I don't see why. Many cheaper houses are built in factories. Haven't you seen OVERSIZE LOADS going down the highways, one half in one vehicle and the other half in another? You can take them wherever you want, put the two sides together, and lo! with a little finishing, you have a house.

OF: Some persons with social consciences - including Quakers that I know - purposely live in mixed neighborhoods, middle-class and poor together. However, others don't want the value of an expensive house decreased because a cheap one is built next door.

JP: Shouldn't zoning be unprejudiced as to the value of houses constructed? If my house loses value because of my neighbor, will not my neighbor's house gain value because of mine? Is he or she any less important to God than I am? As we provide housing for the homeless, should we not be unprejudiced as to where in the city it is located?

OF: Most people don't want poor people living next to them. They play loud music, and they shout at each other in foreign languages.

JP: I sense stereotype. We speak of affirmative action - diversity in education and business - should we not also have affirmative action in neighborhoods?

OF: We do have laws that say no one can be denied the right to buy a house anywhere because of ethnic origin.

JP: True, but we don't say no one can be denied the right to build a house because 'one' can't afford a house like the neighbors'.

OF: Suppose we do give cash subsidies for housing, but the low-income person spends it on drink or drugs. The rest of us have a choice in spending our money. But if we *give* money to a low-income person for some specific purpose, we do not like to see it misspent.

JP: Well, why not give vouchers instead, which can be spent only on housing? The seller or contractor might cash them in with the government.

OF: That method isn't foolproof. False sales might "launder" the vouchers into cash, and public officials can be bribed.

JP: True, but diversion would be lessened, and besides, the low-income person does need a house.

Second Problem: Building Codes

JP: I really see two problems. One is that when we subsidize low-income housing, we deny the poor people the chance to choose their houses and locations. They have to take what we give them. The other is that our building codes are so expensive to comply with that poor people cannot afford modern housing. They are pushed out into the streets.

In Longmont, Colorado, ten miles from our home, we used to buy sweet corn grown and picked by Mexican migrant labor. The corn was delicious. The laborers were provided with housing far better than the shacks they used to inhabit in Mexico, though not as good as neighboring American houses. One day the housing authority declared those houses substandard, and the farmer was ordered to bring them up to code. He could not afford to do so, so the workers were told to live elsewhere. They could not find housing they could afford, and the farmer could not afford to pay higher wages. So they drifted on, and the farm was closed down.

All concerned were harmed, and no one gained. I was harmed the least because I could buy corn elsewhere. Greater harm was done to the farmer, but I presume he could find another job. The greatest of harm was done to the workers, who were left homeless in a strange country.

The other day I was reading a story about migrant labor picking cherries in Oregon:

> Thousands of workers who formerly camped in make-shift but at least convenient camps on growers' farms are now scrambling to find shelter in forests, beside rivers, or in private or state-run campgrounds, many of them far away from the cherry orchards. The reason: federal regulators at the Occupational Safety and Health Administration (OSHA) ruled in May that the growers' camps were not clean or safe enough. But no alternatives have been provided.[1]

Here is still another report:

> Strictly enforcing New York's housing codes would hurt immigrants, not help them. To cut housing costs, some 23% of immigrant households live in crowded conditions, most of which violate city codes. . . If New

York landlords are forced to reduce occupancy levels to code-mandated standards, it will drive thousands - maybe tens of thousands - of immigrants out of their homes. Where would they go? Into the streets, perhaps, or into other crowded quarters elsewhere.[2]

Here's another. A 1999 report by the Housing and Urban Development Agency states that "low-income families find the supply of affordable housing diminishing. Waiting lists are growing, and the length of time families must wait is increasing." [3]

We have high standards for our housing, written into our building codes for both safety and convenience. Electrical wiring must be protected. Insulation must be adequate. Structure must be solid. These codes describe houses of far higher quality than most immigrants from less developed countries live in, as evident from the Longmont farm, from the New York City report on codes, and from the HUD report.

Third Problem: Do the Poor Want to Own Houses?

OF: I've been sitting in silence so far, but now I must speak up. This discussion smacks of the middleclass mindset. You all seem to feel that the homeless want to own houses, and you speak of "affordable housing." As a social worker, I have worked among the homeless. For the most part, owning a house is the last thing on their minds.

JP: What is on their minds, then?

OF: Most of my clients wanted a place to lay their heads and shelter their families. But they have other problems too - poor credit, for example, no job - that make it difficult for them to get good rentals. And rents are so expensive they are priced out of the market. They have to live in places no one else would want.

JP: But so many Quakers talk about affordable housing - meaning to build houses - that they wouldn't believe me if I tell them that homeless people don't want to own houses.

OF: The two problems you raised - about ghettoes and zoning, and building codes, are real problems, but they are not the ones primarily on the minds of street people. Rather, they need shelter in a safe neighborhood - free of drugs and crimes. They need more space for their children, so they don't have to crowd five kids into a bedroom. All this means they need more money. But giving them money won't help. Their lives are so difficult that the result we would be looking for - better housing - wouldn't happen.

JP: I think you're saying that housing is just one tiny aspect of a far greater problem - that of poverty and the way of life associated with it.

OF: Friend, you have finally caught on!

Summary

JP: We now see that "affordable housing" is far more than merely subsidized homes. Of course there is a question of zoning. More important is whether our building codes are pricing the poor out into the streets. Then OF came along and turned the whole discussion on its head. Do the poor want to own houses, she asked? No, they have other things in mind. Welcome, Friends, to the much broader question of poverty. If we wish to tackle housing for the poor, OF says, we have to start elsewhere.

The workshop was puzzled, because poverty seemed too big an issue to tackle in a single afternoon. So, we did what most Quakers do when we can't decide where to go next. We had a period of silence, hoping the Divine Light would guide us.

NOTES

[1] *The Economist,* 7/3/99.
[2] Salins in *New York Times,* 10/26/96.
[3] Havemann in *Washington Post Weekly,* 3/15/99.

Chapter 8

"Forgive the Debts of Poor Countries"

After a moment of silence, JP began the meeting with an announcement:

JP: Throughout the less developed world - in Asia, Africa, and Latin America - countries are so deeply in debt there is no possibility they will ever repay. The interest is staggering and may go on forever. Should we forgive those debts?

From time to time and place to place, debts have been forgiven. Both the Romans and Greeks were known to do it. Forgiving debts is part of the Lord's prayer. We are now faced with the latest proposal for mass forgiveness, named "Jubilee 2000," in the hope that it would occur during that year.

The depth of the problem is seen in the following two quotations:

There are 41 poor nations considered the most highly indebted, 80 percent of them in Africa. Some pay 60 percent of their annual budgets for debt service. That leaves little to invest in basic education, health, rural roads and other programs that help people escape from poverty. Prodded by religious and development groups, the World Bank and the I.M.F. began a program in 1996 to help poor countries reduce their debt.[1]

Adding its voice to a movement that would link the year 2000 with a biblical concept of financial relief for the poor, the World Council of Churches called Monday for canceling the foreign debts of impoverished nations. In adopting the statement the council has aligned itself with a growing number of religious leaders and some secular groups who want to tie the millennium to the ideal of a "jubilee" year. The Book of Leviticus has a visionary description of such a period,

which would occur every 49th year, in which slaves
would be freed, debtors released from their obligations
and land restored to its owners. Drawing on that theme,
the statement, "A Jubilee Call to End the Stranglehold
of Debt on Impoverished Peoples," cites biblical pas-
sages to make the case that a special period of debt
relief for the poor is "as relevant today as it was thousands of years ago."[2]

OF: As a business person, I'd like to point out that some
debts should be honored. Suppose I'm a bank in some more developed country. I receive money from my depositors and invest it in a
factory in Africa that provides jobs to needy Africans. If that debt is
forgiven - so it isn't paid back to me - how am I going to have the
funds to repay my depositors when they want to withdraw? Wouldn't
I say, "I'll never do that again!"

JP: Some say private creditors should be included in Jubilee 2000, but mostly the lenders resist this, for reasons that OF just
mentioned. I believe OF is right. Private debt is a cobweb of obligations, and if it is forgiven, small depositors, stockholders, and others are apt to suffer.

However, mostly the debts are owed to the International
Monetary Fund, the World Bank, and to the governments of seven
industrial countries (known as the G-7). How about forgiving those?
The taxpayers in rich countries would suffer, but they can afford to.

OF: How did these debts arise?

JP: Beginning after World War II and continuing today.
most less developed countries (LDCs) – especially in Africa - have
been ruled by authoritarian governments that have printed new money
through banks,[3] then lent it to their cronies who invested in their pet
projects. Had these projects been successful, their proceeds would
have repaid the debt. But in fact, many pet projects were unsound.
They did not result in goods consumers would buy or in solid infra-
structure.

In many countries, particularly in East Asia, the projects
seemed initially successful, because the government would make

up for losses through further loans. Attracted by this success, private investors poured in foreign money through short-term loans (maturities of only a few months). The interest and dividends on these loans would be paid by additional foreign-denominated loans supplied by later investors, in a pattern known in the West as a Ponzi scheme. As a result, most of the banks in LDCs are now in technical bankruptcy – that is, they would be bankrupt according to the principles of Western society if they were not kept alive by infusions of cash from government.

In order to keep their promises - often to foreign investors - governments borrowed from the IMF, World Bank, and G-7, who always made the condition that the governments cease lending to cronies for unsound projects and that they examine their projects more carefully, and the like. Often the governments did not keep their promises, but the IMF, World Bank, and G-7 would try again, with further loans and further promises, until they ran out of patience. By then, the outstanding balances were horrendous.

Should Friends favor forgiving the debts of these unscrupulous rulers?

OF: Yes, we should. Regardless of whether the rulers are scoundrels, they are keeping their people in thrall when we demand that they repay. They would have no funds left over for the "basic education, health, rural roads and other programs" that JP read about in the quotation.

JP: But what assurance do we have that if debts are forgiven, the governments will indeed spend the money on "basic education, health, rural roads and other programs?"

OF: Applying these funds for the basic programs would be made a condition for forgiveness. Governments would have to sign promises to that effect.

JP: How can we expect governments to honor written promises when they have not done so in the past? Even when they have not been in debt, these governments have neglected their poor, providing minimal or no education and not many other social services. They have also been corrupt and profligate. Once we forgive their debts, is there any reason to believe they will suddenly live up to their promises?

Besides, don't you remember how governments deeply resent Americans telling them what to do? And how it is virtually impossible to make them do what they do not want to do on their own soil?

OF: But what else can we do other than forgive the debt?

JP: We could let them go bankrupt. Many governments have defaulted in their debts, including England in 1348, Spain in the sixteenth century (several times), Russia during 1999, and the United States when it refused to honor its promise to redeem paper money with gold in 1934. Often "bankruptcy" occurs through depreciating the currency until it is worthless, as in Germany during the 1920s, Bolivia in the 1950s, and Argentina in the 1980s.

OF: Wouldn't bankruptcy just have the same effect as forgiving the debt?

JP: No. In bankruptcy the *debtor* declares 'one's' inability to pay, as opposed to the *creditor* forgiving. But bankruptcy and forgiveness would have exactly the same impact on the "basic education, health, rural roads and other programs."

OF: Then why do we hear so much about debt forgiveness? Why would not bankruptcy be preferred?

JP: For several reasons: First, bankruptcy would wound the pride of the IMF, World Bank, and G-7, who would have to explain the poor quality of their loans or to justify other loans in the future. Second, forgiveness implies validation of past practices, so that governments might do them again, expecting more forgiveness. Third, bankruptcy implies lack of creditworthiness, which has indeed been the case but which the international financial world does not want to admit. Fourth, bankrupt governments are apt to be humiliated and overthrown, which they should be. Fifth, foreign investors may think twice about entrusting their funds to bankrupt countries, although in the past they have frequently done so anyway.

So, all the reasons why special interests favor forgiveness over bankruptcy are reasons why Friends should favor the reverse. I favor bankruptcy because I believe the borrowers are mainly scoundrels, who have wasted the funds they have borrowed, and who should be punished rather than rewarded.

[The recording clerk noted that Friends were perplexed. They had a warm feeling toward forgiving the debts of the poor. When told that the debts had been incurred not by the poor but by corrupt, rich, authoritarian rulers, they were not sure whether to believe JP. When JP said these rulers would probably not spend more money on education and social services even if the debts were forgiven, they felt sure that he was hard-hearted. JP, on the other hand, felt that Friends had not adequately understood the cultures of the less developed world, but that they believed LDC governments followed principles similar to those of their own countries, where banks are closely regulated to see that they do not lend for unsound projects, and where a contract is meant to be honored. This - JP averred - was a gross and tragic error.]

NOTES

[1] Editorial in *New York Times,* 4/30/99.
[2] Niehbur in *New York Times,* 12/15/98.
[3] Technically they do not "print" new money but instead open up new bank deposits.

Chapter 9

"Don't Buy the Products of Sweatshops"

"In many parts of Asia, Africa, and Latin America, millions of children, some as young as six, toil for long hours at low or no wages in back-breaking or dangerous jobs, deprived of schooling or of the pleasures of conventional childhood. Many work alongside their parents on farms or in other family businesses; others, less fortunate, are sold into bonded slavery; millions more work in factories or sweatshops producing goods that eventually find their way to shops in London, New York, or Munich."[1]

Since Americans became aware of these conditions in less developed countries in the middle 1990s, numerous reports have appeared from many countries. "On any given day, an estimated 250 million children between the ages of 5 and 14 years work under dirty, hazardous conditions in less developed countries and many more toil as migrant farm workers in industrialized countries. In many cases, work takes the place of school."[2] In India alone, an estimated 40 million to 100 million child laborers are at work, according to a United Nations report.[3] When my workshop participants were reminded that much of the apparel they were wearing was manufactured by sweatshop labor, they were incensed and immediately wanted to boycott the companies selling it.

In this, they were at one with many activist groups in the United States, particularly college students who wanted their universities to foreswear the purchase of college insignia from companies using sweatshop labor. As the movement spread, a citizens' Economic Priorities Accreditation Agency was set up to establish standards for social accountability of multinational corporations and grant them certificates of compliance. Manufacturers joined in. "After more than two years of debate, a group of human rights organizations and apparel manufacturers, including Nike, Reebok, and Liz Claiborn, . . . reached an agreement intended to curtail sweatshops by setting up a code of conduct and a monitoring system for overseas factories used by American companies."[4] Working together with a White House task force, they agreed that "American manufacturers pledge not to do business with companies that use forced labor or require employees to work more than 60 hours a week."[5] The association was joined by 56 colleges whose administrators promised not to use sweatshop products in college insignia.[6]

The White House made several strong statements in favor of the compact. President Clinton announced "a large increase in funding for programs to stop child labor around the world."[7]

Just as the agreement was being put into effect, university students protested that it was not strong enough. Students at Duke and Georgetown held "raucous protests" in January 1999.[8] They were joined by students at Harvard, Brown, and other universities.[9] Late in 1999 students from Columbia, Duke, Notre Dame, Wisconsin, and other institutions formed the Workers' Rights Consortium, which would "alleviate sweatshop conditions by inspecting apparel factories worldwide."[10]

My Friends' workshops were all eager to form solidarity with these students, until I raised some queries. Here is the conversation that ensued:

JP: Millions of poor families in less developed countries depend on the labor of their children for their very subsistence. If the children are fired, the family might starve. "As a result of American pressure, perhaps 30,000 children have been thrown out of their jobs in [Bangladesh's] textile industry in the past two years. A study by Oxfam, a British charity, found that far from going to school, many of these children have ended up in far more dangerous employment, in welding shops or in prostitution."[11]

The New York Times tells this story: "A quarter-billion children 14 and under work worldwide. Unicef estimates that fewer than 1 in 20 make goods for export — and those who do are the most fortunate working children. The vast majority are employed in far more harmful occupations. Children in agriculture are poisoned by pesticides. Prostitutes get AIDS. Miners and glassworkers inhale dangerous substances. Shoe shiners and gum sellers are at the mercy of the streets. Domestic servants live in isolation and suffer beatings and sexual abuse. Millions of children in South Asia are sold by their parents into bonded labor to work off family debts."[12]

Here's another case. "West Bengal [India] creates child beggars for export. In return for payments ranging from $75 to $1,500 and more to their parents, children are handed over to touts, equipped with false passports representing them as the touts' children, and taken 3,000 miles to beg in the streets of Saudi Arabia. Some are as young as 4, the oldest about 15."[13]

How would you feel about forcing a sweatshop to close down if the children who worked there were forced into these other atrocities?

OF: I don't want sweatshops to close. I would be willing to pay a higher price for my shoes if I knew the workers who made them were paid higher wages and enjoyed clean working conditions.

JP: How would you be sure that would happen?

OF: We would send monitors to examine the factories our products were coming from.

JP: You've heard of the "Ugly American" - Americans who tell other countries how their people ought to live. Often Americans have demanded that other governments award favorable access, taxes, privileges, etc. to our multinational corporations. Remember that "sweatshops" are the way of life in many countries around the world. Don't they resent Americans interfering with their businesses of whatever kind?

OF: They would have to agree, if they wanted to sell us their goods.

JP: But would the host countries wonder why the United States should want to improve labor conditions in just a few factories exporting to the United States, when millions of other factories have the same conditions?

Then, suppose we *could* promote better working conditions in those few factories. Would we be setting up an elite class of workers compared to those in the millions of other factories in the same country who would not have the same privileges?

OF: We have to start somewhere. At least we could tell them how we feel about goods they sell us.

JP: Good point. However, before you reached your opinion on the issue of child labor in less developed countries, did you (or someone you trust) ask the workers themselves, or their families, how *they* feel about it? Here's a report from Honduras: "With wages that start at less than 40 cents an hour, the apparel plants offer little by American standards. But many of the people who work in them, having come from jobs that pay even less, see employment here as the road to a better life."[14]

My next question is whether you have all the facts. *The New York Times* reports that in 1999, a class action suit against garment factories in Saipan, a South Pacific island under the jurisdiction of the United States, charged that "in dozens of factories . . . workers are forced to work inhuman hours and to live in overcrowded and vermin-infested conditions . . . that the workers are enduring a form of slavery, trapped with impossible debts and with little freedom to leave Saipan. . . But interviews with dozens of Chinese workers here tell a story that is not so stark. Chatting easily as they stroll freely in the evening after work, they describe orderly factories and clean dormitories, a view borne out in visits. They say they come to Saipan voluntarily to earn about five times what they made in China, heading home after two years with $6,000 to $10,000 saved."[15]

I grieve with you about working conditions in less developed countries. *I know what they are like, because I have been there.* I have walked through the slums of many countries in Asia, Africa, and Latin America, talked to slumdwellers, and have seen their shacks. I have been in factories in Latin America and India and have talked with their workers. I think American interference is more likely to cause sweatshop workers to lose their best means of livelihood, horrible though it may be. This shows the kind of world in which we live. We can't patch it up with boycotts here and there. A few lifetimes of service are necessary.

[The recording clerk noted that the workshop was in unity that labor conditions in less developed countries were despicable, even tragic. Both JP and all the OFs agreed we should not rest until these were changed. But the workshop was not in unity on what to do. JP felt strongly that no boycott should occur unless the sweatshop workers had themselves been consulted and had agreed. A boycott, he said, would set into motion a chain of events whose outcome we don't know, but which would likely push the children into greater atrocities than they now face. He also thought that instead of boycotting sweatshops, we should buy as much as possible from them, so they would have to hire more laborers, paying higher wages to attract them. This is what happened in Hong Kong and Singapore, he said, where wages quintupled in just one generation. Some OFs felt they could not, in good conscience, wear the products of sweatshop labor, no matter what. Most agreed that the issue was very complicated and needed further study. (A few thought that "further study" was an excuse for inaction, however). Although the workshop did not end in unity on its major points, JP's questions, the willingness of OFs to listen to them, and his willingness to listen to their replies, showed that all were seeking the truth.]

NOTES

[1] *The Economist,* 6/3/95.
[2] *New York Times,* editorial, 12/31/96.
[3] *New York Times,* 10/24/98.
[4] *New York Times,* 11/5/98.
[5] *Wall Street Journal,* 11/6/98.
[6] *New York Times,* 4/25/99.
[7] *New York Times,* 12/10/98.
[8] *New York Times,* 1/31/99.
[9] *New York Times,* 4/25/99.
[10] *New York Times,*10/20/99.
[11] *New York Times,* 2/20/00.
[12] *The Economist,* 6/3/95.
[13] *New York Times,* 3/13/97.
[14] *New York Times,* 7/18/96.
[15] *New York Times,* 2/20/99.

Chapter 10

"44 Million Americans Don't Have Health Insurance"

Forty four million Americans do not have health insurance. If one of them faces catastrophic illness and family funds run out, the patient may die. Friends in my workshops found this condition to be unacceptable in a country as rich as ours. I thought so, too.

I thought of 1992, when our 37-year-old daughter, Cindy, was diagnosed with stomach cancer. Her bills were paid by health insurance. But as she lay dying, I lay sleepless with demons flying around my head. Suppose some cure had a 5% probability of success, but it would cost all our assets - house, car, retirement savings - and put us deeply into debt. Would we do it? We would face a 95% probability of ending up destitute after losing our daughter. If we did not, how could we live with ourselves? The 44 million without health insurance could face just that monstrosity.

In our cancer support group, we met Courtney Klee, a vibrant 20-year-old university student who had a serious cancer. A bone marrow transplant was her only hope, but her insurance company would not pay because it was "experimental." Courtney solicited her friends - Robin and I contributed - and the Boulder papers screamed headlines, seeking more funds. Money poured in, the insurance company was shamed into paying the rest, Courtney had her transplant, and then she died. Why should a dying Courtney be put to all that trauma in a rich country like ours? Will a rich country pay horrendous bills when the probability of life is slim?

Friends were baffled by these questions. One said he would give up 90% of his income and live like a pauper if we could have universal health coverage. Others were not so sure of the amount, but they would make sacrifices. Then we ran into the problem of democracy.

Democracy a problem? Yes, because our Friend's 90% would be a drop in the bucket. Others would have to match it, and they won't. In a democracy, we cannot force others to our will. Some Friends said we should devote our entire military budget to health care (and maybe to education and a few other benefits) - pacifist me thought so too - but citizens in a democracy would not vote for that. So, what should Friends favor?

Should the government provide health care for Bill Gates? "Yes," said one Friend. "The rich are as much in my heart as the poor." Others, including me, agreed that they are in our hearts, but that did not mean we should pay for their health care any more than we buy groceries for them.

Cindy died in Rochester, N.Y., four months after diagnosis. During the long, agonizing wait, I heard her doctors complain that they were overloaded with cases from Canada, whose border lay only eighty miles away. "I hear the vast majority of Canadians are happy with their health insurance," I said to Cindy's oncologist. "The vast majority of Canadians do not have serious cancer" was his terse reply.

Seven years later, in 2000, *The New York Times* reported as follows on the Canadian health care system. I'm sorry the quotation is so long, but if you are thinking of a single-payer system, it is worth reading:[1]

> In Toronto, Canada's largest city, overcrowding prompted emergency rooms in 23 of the city's 25 hospitals to turn away ambulances one day last week. Two weeks ago, in what one newspaper later called an "ominous foreshadowing," police officers shot to death a distraught father who had taken a doctor hostage in a Toronto emergency room in an attempt to speed treatment for his sick baby.

> Further west, in Winnipeg, "hallway medicine" has become so routine that hallway stretcher locations have permanent numbers. Patients recuperate more slowly in the drafty, noisy hallways, doctors report.

> On the Pacific Coast, ambulances filled with ill patients have repeatedly stacked up this winter in the park-

ing lot of Vancouver General Hospital. Maureen Whyte, a hospital vice president, estimates that 20 percent of heart attack patients who should have treatment within 15 minutes now wait an hour or more.

The shortage is a case of supply not keeping up with demand. During the 1990's, after government deficits ballooned, partly because of rising health costs, the government in Ottawa cut revenue-sharing payments to provinces — by half, by some accounts. Today, the federal budget is balanced, but 7 hospitals in Montreal have been closed, and 44 hospitals in Ontario have been closed or merged.

The Economist carried a similar report about Britain's health care system in 2000: "Survival rates from some serious diseases are poor. According to researchers at the London School of Economics (LSE), British women under 65 who are diagnosed with breast cancer have one of the worst survival rates in Western Europe. And a British woman with heart disease is four times more likely to be killed by it than a woman with the same disease living in France."[2]

I thought back on my professional visits to nineteen Latin American, sixteen African, and four Asian countries, where I have always done two things: (1) ask my professional counterparts, usually in the government or universities, how the government is living up to its promises on social welfare; and (2) wander through the slums, talking to the poor at random, asking the same question. Whether professionals or slumdwellers, the answers were the same: all promises, little action. Before writing *The Moral Economy,* I studied the health care systems of Canada, Britain, and all European countries, Here are some quotations from that book:[3]

France. "Its spending of nearly FFR 2 trillion a year - more than the entire state budget - has been spiraling out of control."

Denmark. "Waiting lists for routine hospital operations are irritatingly long, and newspapers detail many horror stories about the state of the country's hospitals."

Italy. "Reports abound of insufficient care, misdiagnoses, unnecessary deaths, and unsanitary conditions. Protests in Naples centered on 'fleas in the bed, fecal traces in the fish.'"

Poland. "Waiting periods are very long: drugs, equipment, and facilities are inadequate; there are not enough beds and specialist services; and patient relations with physicians and other health care workers are poor."

Formerly Communist region: "Financially strapped governments have neglected health care and now face what experts are calling an unprecedented crisis."

Japan. "Clinics are crowded, with long waiting periods. A Japanese friend tells me that the sheets were not changed during the week she spent in the hospital for a minor ear operation."

In the *United States,* we have an employer-insurance system, but it has many defects. It gives benefits to employed people that unemployed do not enjoy. It encourages employers to hire part-time labor or contractors instead of full-time, because these are not subject to health insurance - the accounting would be too complicated. The terms of the contract are decided between the employer and the insurance company, whereas (to my thinking) the employee should have that choice and that responsibility. Why do we not divorce health insurance from the employer, pay the insurance cost direct to the employee as an increment in salary, and have each employee make 'one's' own contract with the insurance company?

For several reasons. First, because unions have opposed it. Unions, representing mainly full-time employees, want to keep the advantage that their members have over part-timers. A second reason is that employers are believed to have more clout than individual workers in negotiating insurance contracts. (This could be remedied by insurance clubs with the same clout.) But the most compelling reason - I believe - is that we are in a national mood for collective over personal responsibility, the kind of mood that changes only over centuries.

Collective or personal responsibility was a hot topic in all my meetings with Friends. Many thought that with collective responsibility we lovingly join with others to do cooperatively what individuals cannot do separately. They were partial toward communes, where one cares for all and all for one. While I favor communes if they are voluntary, I thought the outside world would demand compulsion. There, collective responsibility would call upon individuals to delegate functions to a government that imposes its collective will upon individuals. I believe individual choices, differing from person to person, would be preferred.

Let me propose a system of health care in which all citizens would be required to have minimum medical insurance from birth, just as we are required to have automobile insurance in most states. Those who cannot afford the minimum would be subsidized from public funds - *but only those.* Insurance would be by contract between insurance company and insured, with a wide variety of choices above the minimum. If a patient has a condition not covered by 'one's' contract, 'one' would pay for the treatment or choose not to have it. If the condition is life-threatening and the patient cannot pay, the public treasury would do so, to be repaid by the patient over time or from 'one's' estate.[4]

This is a compassionate system that nurtures personal responsibility. Some insurance companies would provide - at a cost - policies that would pay for catastrophic-illness treatment with a 95% probability of failure; others would not. I believe the choice should be individual, not the same for all, nor should it be made by Congress and the President.

Our nation is in a historical period in which it is widely believed that benefits should be provided by government. The result - I believe - is that personal responsibility is weakened and ultimately, as in the Canadian health care system, the services are not adequately supplied.

Not many Friends were persuaded. Among Friends, the collective responsibility ethic is strongly held. I did not try to dissuade them, because I believe history will dissuade them over the next century. I hope Friends will consider once again the Quaker virtue of individual responsibility and voluntary cooperation, which belong to our religious heritage from the seventeenth century. (Remember Chapter 2, by Gusten Lutter).

NOTES

[1]Brooke, James, "Full Hospitals Make Canadians Wait and Look South," January 16, 2000.

[2] *The Economist,* 1/22/00.

[3] These quotations are taken from pages 93-97, where the cases are discussed in greater detail.

[4] This proposal is described in greater detail in *The Moral Economy,* pp.90-97.

Chapter 11

"Social Security Isn't Enough"

SCENE: The same twenty Friends as in Chapter 6. To invoke discussion, JP played devil's advocate, opening with a startling statement.

JP: Let us abolish government social security.

OF (shocked): Hundreds of thousands of poor elderly depend on government social security. A Quaker should not deprive them of their livelihood and throw them into the streets.

JP: I didn't mean that. I believe our society is rich enough so that no one should be deprived in old age. But you did say they *depend* on government social security. As a Quaker, I seek a world of love, compassion, responsibility, and *interdependency.* Each retiree should have 'one's' own account, which could not be diminished by Congress and the President as is the case with social security. Being dependent is something like a slave relying on 'one's' master for 'one's' livelihood.

OF: Social security beneficiaries have paid their quotas all their working lives. They are only getting back what they put in. Even that is not enough for a decent livelihood.

JP: I have paid social security taxes all my working life, and my funds have all been blown up over Vietnam, Iraq, Bosnia, and Kosovo, and here I am a pacifist. The Social Security Trust Fund contains only IOUs from the government. My social security check is financed by current younger workers. By about 2015, when the baby boomers retire, there won't be enough younger ones to support them.

OF: What do you mean by "responsibility and interdepency?"

JP: To be responsible and interdependent, I think workers should personally save for their retirement. Instead of paying taxes, they would be required by law to invest the same amounts in money market certificates, mutual funds, bonds, or savings accounts, over which they would have control. Thus they would be interdependent with the companies in which they invest.

As a nation, we have forgotten how to save. Net personal savings are now zero or close to it if credit card debts are counted as negative saving. We have abdicated to government what should be a personal responsibility.

OF: But many individuals don't know how to select good investments.

JP: That's where Quakers might help. Saving would be taught in schools, and we would set up advisory services for adult workers. We might also require by law that what is now paid in social security taxes would be invested only in blue chip mutual funds.

OF: But even they might crash.

JP: You are right; that is a risk. But compare it to the risk that taxpayers will refuse to fund the government enough to pay social security thirty years hence. In any thirty-year period in the history of our country, investments in blue chips have always come out ahead, even including years of market crash. Universities and insurance companies invest in blue chips, and their endowments don't fail. Don't they have a better record on risk than even the government does?

These investments depend on the productive capacity of our companies, not on how much Congress demands in taxes. During all our history as a nation, we have been productive, and currently our productivity (output per unit of labor) is among the highest in the world. It is out of this productivity that investments pay dividends and increase in value. There is no reason for that to change.

OF: I've heard that retirees get back more in social security than they paid in taxes.

JP: In some cases, yes, but those estimates depend on alternative possibilities. If instead of social security taxes, workers invest in savings accounts at 3% a year, then they would have gotten more back in social security. But if they invest in blue chips, they will do better than social security would have. Also, remember that every government offering social security has reneged on some of its promises, including the United States. Congress and the President could abolish social security without paying a penny back if they dared politically. But investments in companies are contracts, enforceable at law.

OF: But suppose a worker is tempted by speculative funds and loses all 'one's' investment.

JP: In a society based on Quaker principles, we take responsibility for our actions. If you gamble, be prepared to lose.

OF: Yes, but what about the children of such a loser? They aren't responsible.

JP: To take care of them and their parents, we will have a Welfare program, which will be the subject of Chapter 12.

OF: What about workers who don't earn enough to save for an adequate retirement?

JP: Remember that in our health-care meeting, I suggested that the poor should be subsidized. Same for social security. Low-income workers should receive money from the public treasury so they may invest in approved funds just like anyone else.

OF: How much?

JP: That we will decide democratically, but it should never be so much that workers do not have incentive to be promoted off the subsidy list.

If you believe the government should supply social security, you are certainly in keeping with the national ethic, and I respect your opinions. But I believe that over the next century, that ethic will be forced to change. In any welfare state, citizens always want to take more out of the pot than they are willing to put in, and they cannot. As benefits are canceled, social unrest will follow. I hope that instead of demanding more and more for our favorites - the disadvantaged - Quakers will be in the foreground of reconciling the adversaries.

Indeed, the future has already arrived in Germany, and it is not good. Social programs already cost far more than citizens are willing to pay. Businesses are fleeing Germany because of taxes more than twice as high as in the United States. They leave behind a lower tax base and many unemployed.

Instead of paying taxes as they would if they had jobs, Germany's unemployed cost the government funds for their welfare. When the government tries to cut the benefits to balance the budget, the unemployed riot and students strike. As this book is written, no one knows how the German problem will be resolved. But it is serious, even grave, all the more so because of Germany's otherwise powerful position in Europe. The United States is far from matching Germany's predicament now, but it might in fifty years if our ethic doesn't change.

In the preceding three paragraphs, I spoke as an economist. Now let me talk as a Quaker. To my thinking, my proposal to abolish government social security and substitute a private system is a Quakerly way. First, it still provides social security for all. Second, it encourages individual responsibility, a Quaker virtue. Third, it places two safety nets under the poor - the subsidy for those unable to pay for the minimum required investments, and the welfare system for those who either meet unusual misfortune or recklessly squander their assets. Fourth, it could be put into effect immediately, if only it enjoyed enough popular support. Fifth, it adheres to Quaker simplicity, compared to the complex, convoluted proposals currently being made by Congress. Finally, it thinks in the long run, not just about what will happen tomorrow.

Let us now have a moment of silence. Tomorrow, if Friends wish, we will talk about Welfare.

[*NOTE:* This discussion did not actually happen. Rather, it is a synthesis of conversations I have had with Friends, sometimes singly and sometimes as part of discussions on other topics. When she saw the draft of this chapter, one Friend thought I had regressed into my classroom mode, to educate on what social security is. I was trying to "persuade," she said, not "seek truth together." I did not rewrite the chapter, however, because I could think of no other way to present the message. Have I regressed to my mode before the "road to Damascus" (see Chapter 1)? Was I seeking the truth together with other Friends, or was I presumptuous to think I already had it? You judge.]

Chapter 12

"The Welfare System Has Made the Poor Poorer"

SCENE: Same as yesterday, with same characters. After the open-ing silence, OF was led to speak:

OF: Our welfare system has made the poor poorer. After keeping them dependent for many years, the Welfare Act of 1996 demands that recipients find jobs. It sets a time limit of five years: Work or Out!

JP: That's right. The act does not distinguish between those able to work and those unable, because of drug addiction, family problems, child care, poor health, or any other reason. It's often touted as a success because welfare rolls have been greatly reduced, but the move has left many in poverty, including children, because they cannot find jobs when they are kicked off.

Jason deParle is a *New York Times* reporter who sees pov-erty at a ground level. For example, Lashanda Washington is a 20-year old capable of getting and holding jobs, who nevertheless lost them through devotion to her mother. Her mother "has staggered drunk in the streets and been hit by a car; checked into a psychiatric ward; weathered immobilizing outbreaks of herpes; and started many days crying to her family that she fears she is dying."

> Skipping work to keep watch at home, Lashanda has found herself trapped in irreconcilable roles: breadwinner, daugh-ter, confidant, playmate, social worker, nurse and cop. She wakes her mother and chides her to eat; buys her beer when she gets the shakes; and searches the alleys when she dis-appears.[1]

What should our society do about Lashanda?

OF: She should be off welfare and her mother on.

JP: But her mother requires far more attention than Welfare can pay her. So, should Lashanda abandon her mother so she can make her own life?

(Friends thought so, but they recognized that it was Lashanda's choice and consequences. They saw no solution for the mother).

DeParle writes of many cases similar to Lashanda's, where an intense loyalty toward a dysfunctional family intrudes upon the ability of an able-bodied worker to keep a job. The worker no longer qualifies for welfare, and the family problems are more than any agency can handle.

OF: On the other hand, the government takes care of lots of people who don't need it. I read of a father who took his kids to a baby sitter whom the government paid $1,390 a year from the School Lunch Act, when he could have afforded that himself.[2] Welfare should drop everyone that does not really need the support.

OF: But we're a rich nation. We could easily afford the tiny amount we were spending on welfare. I'd rather support a few people avoiding work than push mentally incapacitated ones into the streets.

JP: The Cato Institute in Washington studied welfare in the entire country, showing that if recipients took advantage of all programs - Aid for Dependent Children, Supplemental Security Income, food stamps, Medicaid, housing, nutrition assistance, and energy assistance, in most cases they could get more from the government than from a private employer. Considering that welfare payments are not taxed, the equivalent hourly wage ranged from $5.53 in Mississippi to $17.50 in Hawaii. In 39 states and DC, welfare pays more than $8 per hour.[3] So, of course many recipients prefer welfare to work.

I believe, however, that those are the ones who in fact found jobs when they were forced to.

OF: Wait a bit! I'm unclear on where to go from here if I don't know how the system works now.

JP: I was hoping someone would ask. The act of 1996 devolved welfare upon the states, with federal financial help. Each state might adopt its own program, just so long as it met the federal requirement to place a rising percentage of welfare participants into work, at first for 20 hours a week and later for 30.[4]

Each state has operated a bit differently. Several began their programs before the federal law went into effect. In California the welfare check was reduced so that welfare pays less than part-time work at minimum wage.[5] In Virginia, welfare recipients signed "personal responsibility contracts" requiring them to begin work within 90 days; their communities offered them jobs.[6] Michigan relaxed rules requiring recipients to go off welfare when they acquired jobs.[7] In Connecticut, parents were allowed to earn incomes up to the poverty level before they lost their welfare checks.[8]

Wisconsin stopped giving cash to able-bodied applicants but instead put them into private-sector jobs, to be subsidized if need be.[9] Dividing recipients into those truly unable to work and those able, the state still paid those who could not find jobs but required them to do community service if they could.[10] A lifetime limit of five years within the system is set, and health care and child care are provided.[11] Counselors spend several hours with each claimant, to examine alternatives to public assistance: trial jobs, permanent jobs, training, and so on. "Uniquely among the states, Wisconsin lets lone mothers keep the child support they receive from the father."[12]

By reading *The New York Times, Wall Street Journal, Washington Post,* and *The Economist* for many years, I have accumulated twenty-five articles describing the failure of welfare reform. Let me read a sample of excerpts, some of which are direct quotations and others paraphrases:

> A sizable portion of welfare recipients are considered by experts to be so poorly skilled or hampered by other problems that they are unlikely to find and keep jobs, no matter how hard they look and even when they face a loss of benefits.[13]

> Important new studies have undermined the faith that welfare experts have had in traditional job-training programs. Receiving a GED [General Education Diploma] does not seem to raise a mother's employability, or functional literacy.[14]

Welfare-to-Work Plans show [that] success is difficult to achieve. Many persons simply cannot adapt to the discipline of the work place.[15]

135,000 children will be struck from disability benefit rolls under the Welfare Act of 1996, or 14% of all poor children who now receive benefits. Most have mental or behavioral problems.

The 1996 act chops away about $50 billion by stripping some disabled children of cash assistance, legal immigrants of medical assistance and childless adults who cannot find work or food stamps - provisions that have nothing to do with creating work but everything to do with balancing the budget by cutting programs for the poor.[16]

Decades of research have shown that financial incentives, such as letting welfare recipients keep more of their benefits when they get jobs, do little to coax people from welfare to work.

A vast majority of people who have dropped off New York State's rapidly-shrinking welfare rolls have not obtained legitimate jobs.[17]

Tens of thousands of families are being forced off welfare as punishment for not complying with tough new rules.[18]

OF: But aren't there *any* successes?

JP: I think there are. The first official data from the U.S. government says that most states were meeting the work requirement, that 25% of recipients had to have jobs by the end of 1998.[19] In addition, 28% of adults still on welfare were doing work of some sort. Doesn't that mean we're getting there, slowly?

Here are a few more excerpts:

The program, "Pathways to Independence," an intensive training program run by Marriott International, places great weight on building self-confidence, but it also covers more mundane skills. Participants are taught how to be interviewed for a job, how to be reliable employees, and how to manage a bank account. They also get work experience. Those who graduate are guaranteed a job. Over 90% of those who start the classes finish them, and almost 80% of those people hold their jobs after a year. . . In his state-of-the-union message [in 1997] . . . President Clinton mentioned five other companies - Sprint, Monsanto, UPS, Burger King and United Airlines - as leaders of a private-sector effort to create jobs for welfare recipients.[20]

The nonprofit Foundation for International Community Assistance (Finca) has programs that help the poor finance, launch and run their own businesses. In 1992 the Aspen Institute counted 108 microenterprise development programs in 38 states.[21]

Prodded by the Welfare to Work Partnership, a nonprofit organization, . . . companies are connecting with community groups to recruit, train and hire welfare parents for entry-level jobs. . . Beginning early in 1997, the partnership initially signed up about 3,200 companies to hire an estimated 135,000 welfare enrollees for entry-level jobs. About three-fourths of the hires are for full-time jobs with health-care benefits. The program has now expanded to about 7,500 companies.[22]

Greater West Town, a neighborhood group in Chicago, takes poorly-educated welfare recipients and other jobless people from the neighborhood and within a few months places almost all of them in steady jobs with possibilities for promotion. The program's distinguishing feature is its focus on the specific training needs of nearby woodworking firms and distribution centers. It also provides mentoring for trainees whose poor work habits and spotty employment records make them unattractive to many employers.[23]

JP: How do you feel about private enterprise running welfare programs?

OF: My leading tells me that only a government should do it, state or federal.

JP: I sympathize with your leading. The few private-enterprise programs we now have are largely subsidized. Marriott pays $5,000 per participant for training, half of which is supplied from public funds. Even so, they just break even. Besides, they don't train many - only 600 from 1991 to 1997.[24] When unions protested "against companies seeking profits from the privatization of welfare, the Clinton Administration blocked a plan that would have allowed businesses a new role in administering social-service programs in Texas."[25]

Wisconsin, too, has relied on private agencies, with very mixed results:

> Administrative problems were just what the state was trying to avoid when it privatized the program — called Wisconsin Works or W-2 — in Milwaukee County, which accounts for 87 percent of the state's 11,000 welfare cases. But despite the effort to import business-world efficiencies, many of those in the program describe their caseworkers as distant and distracted figures who neglect to return phone calls rather than the partners in self-sufficiency depicted in state manuals. Many recipients find themselves bouncing between part-time or temporary jobs, suffering income gaps that planners failed to anticipate.

Privatized programs are never completely privatized - and that is one of their failings. Always there are government supervisors of some sort. In Wisconsin, "the state's offer of subsidized child care, a crucial support service, has foundered on the confusion between rival agencies, one public, the others private, whose staffs and computers often fail to communicate."[26]

I would propose a system in which *completely private* "betterment agencies" would recruit clients from among former welfare recipients. These recipients themselves would choose their agencies and could not legally be turned down. As in housing, social security, and health care, the poor would now be endowed with choices they never had before. For every welfare client, an agency would list a separate set of goals, such as finding a job that the client would keep for a year, or solving family or drug problems, or something else. It would receive a government grant based on estimated cost to achieve those goals, plus a percentage of profit. If the agency accomplishes its work in less than expected time, it earns a profit; if greater than expected time, it incurs a loss.

A separate Welfare Agency would be established for those clients who, for reasons beyond their or the betterment agencies' control, can never hold a job. Lashanda's mother would be one. These clients would be kept on indefinitely, since our country is rich enough to take care of them.

All welfare-type programs - Aid for Dependent Children, Supplemental Security Income, food stamps, Medicaid, housing, nutrition assistance, and energy assistance - would be subsumed under these two types of agencies. Thus the proliferation glut would be controlled.

OF: Why do you think that would work?

JP: I'm not sure it will, but it's the best thought I have. A private betterment agency will watch its clients go elsewhere if it does not serve them well. If the agency does serve clients well, however, it will earn a profit. My main concern would be whether the bureaucracy that supplies the funds could keep its operating hands off. I also shudder at the wrangling that might occur in estimating goals and costs.

Yet, the possibility of an agency going out of business would be a step forward. Public welfare agencies, on the other hand, never go out of business, no matter how poorly they treat their clients, and no matter what their rate of success or failure.

OF: That sounds persuasive, but I'm still not ready to accept a society motivated by profit.

JP: I plan to bring up the economic role of profit in Chapter 15. For now, let's see what we have agreed. I believe the Sense of the Meeting is that those who can work should, those who cannot but are trainable should be trained, including the mildly retarded, and jobs should be found for them. Those who are totally unable - such as the severely retarded or those with intractable other problems - should be cared for. It may not have dawned on us yet what an enormous and costly job it will be to put these principles into effect.

We should humbly remember that even those welfare recipients who have found jobs have not necessarily solved their personal problems. In *The New York Times,*[27] Jason de Parle writes poignantly of former welfare recipients who have jobs but are still enmeshed in problems of family, violence, drugs, and the like. The whole matter of poverty lies far beyond the range of welfare.

We haven't agreed on where the responsibility lies - with government or private agencies - or who should pay the cost, or how much. Nor have we barely touched the overwhelming problems of people in poverty. So, we are not in unity. If we have been seeking the truth together, we may be infinitesimally closer. Let us not give ourselves credit for more than that.

Shall we close with a moment of silence?

NOTES

[1] *New York Times,* 7/4/99.
[2] *Wall Street Journal,* 12/1/94.
[3] *Wall Street Journal,* 9/28/95.
[4] *New York Times,* 5/31/97.
[5] *Wall Street Journal,* editorial, 8/23/95.
[6] *Washington Post National Weekly,* 10/9/95.

[7] *New York Times,* 10/24/95.

[8] *New York Times,* 12/20/95.

[9] *New York Times,* editorial, 5/3/96.

[10] *Wall Street Journal,* 3/6/97.

[11] *The Economist,* 6/22/96.

[12] *The Economist,* 11/1/97.

[13] *Washington Post National Weekly,* 5/15/95.

[14] *Washington Post National Weekly,* 2/28/96.

[15] *New York Times,* 9/1/96.

[16] *New York Times,* editorial, 5/18/97.

[17] *New York Times,* 3/23/98.

[18] *Washington Post National Weekly,* 3/30/98.

[19] *New York Times,* 12/30/98.

[20] *The Economist,* 3/8/97.

[21] *Wall Street Journal,* 1/21/97.

[22] *New York Times,* 11/26/98.

[23] *New York Times,* 8/26/99.

[24] *The Economist,* 3/8/97.

[25] *New York Times,* 5/11/97; *The Economist,* 5/17/99; *Washington Post National Weekly,* 5/19/97.

[26] *New York Times,* 10/18/98.

[27] 12/30/99.

Chapter 13

"Schools in Inner Cities Have Failed"

SCENE: Again the Valiant Twenty.

OF: American schools are sorely divided between rich and poor. Public schools have not been the social levelers they started out to be. Teachers in inner-city schools are not well prepared for their jobs. The kids get away with murder because teachers can't discipline them. They bring guns and drugs to school. They have been known to kill their schoolmates. But rich families, who live in the suburbs, usually have good public schools or send their kids to private ones.

OF: Inner-city schools are underfunded. More money is spent in rich suburbs than in poor cities. Some schools have dropped extracurricular activities, debating teams, and sports, because of budget shortfalls. In New York, one school had to be closed because it was structurally unsound.

JP: Money is the easiest apparent solution, so Americans typically look to money first. But in most cities, school funding per pupil has been increasing for at least two decades, often in excess of inflation. Virtually all elective officials, from the President on down, want to throw more money at the schools. Yet this seems to do no good. The problems remain or increase. Why?

OF: James Traub, who has studied schools extensively, points out that "a child living in an inner city is in school only so many hours. It's the rest of the day - as well as the rest of the neighborhood - that's the big influence, and the big problem."[1]

OF: He is saying - and I agree - that "money spent on schools . . . cannot bridge the abyss between the children of middle-class and poor parents; for poor children grow up in a world without books and stimulating games and where their natural curiosity is regularly squashed and they are isolated from life beyond their neighborhoods."[2]

JP: It seems that what we learn in this session is not going to move the mountain. But, *given* that the major problems arise elsewhere, we still have the question: do we need charter schools or vouchers for private schools? Or should we reform the public schools? Or both?

OF: If we create alternative schools, the best students will abandon the public schools, leaving only the least motivated, whose parents don't care. The poorest of the poor will face even fewer opportunities than before. We have to tackle the problems within the public schools, not enable students to leave them.

OF: Could you explain what charter schools and vouchers are? How do they work?

JP: Good question. In a 1999 survey by Public Agenda, a nonpartisan educational organization, about two-thirds of Americans sampled knew little or nothing of charter schools or vouchers, even in cities where they are practiced.[3]

Charter schools function independently of school boards or other government authority and are not required to follow standardized curricula, textbooks, or other rules. They operate under charter from a state or school board or (in Michigan) a university. They are financed by taxes, charge no tuition, and are open to all who wish to enroll, within the limits of their capacity. "Nearly all charter schools have waiting lists. They are sought out not by parents of privileged children but by families least well served by conventional schools."[4]

While charter schools have been controversial, my impression is that they have, on balance, been successful. Questions that challenge them are: "Has creating them forced public schools to improve [because of the competition]? Are parents of charter-school students more satisfied than they were before? Are charter schools truly public, or are they publicly-financed semi-private schools that have agendas inimical to the public good [such as proselytizing]? The first New York groups to indicate a desire to set up charter schools were religious."[5] The jury is still out on all these questions.

On the other hand, demand for charter schools has been enormous from underprivileged school districts. A news item from Mesa, Arizona, shows parents joining overnight queues, with their names on lotteries, to place their children in schools with back-to-basics education. Four back-to-basics charter schools were opened, to satisfy the demand.[6] "A University of Michigan study of the state's school-choice program found that the spread of charter schools and interdistrict transfers has created new educational opportunities for many of the neediest families . . ."[7]

OF: What about vouchers?

JP: Vouchers are certificates, each carrying a certain sum - often in the neighborhood of $2,000 or $2,500 - enabling the recipient to spend that much on a semester's tuition in a private school. Any shortfall must be paid by the family. States differ in terms and amounts offered. Sometimes vouchers may be used for supplies for home-taught pupils.

OF: Do students get a better education when they use vouchers to go to private schools?

JP: I don't know. Some studies show that voucher students advance under the system, others that they do not. Each researcher criticizes the studies of the others as faulty.[8]

OF: I'm opposed to using public funds for vouchers unless they exclude religious schools. Often vouchers are used to send pupils to parochial (Catholic) schools, where religion is taught. The American Civil Liberties Union opposes vouchers because of the constitutional separation of church and state.

OF: The ACLU should be promoting choice, not opposing it. We have Quaker schools that hold Friends' Meetings, and religion is taught in many private schools. I suspect they proselytize. So it seems to be all right for the schools that rich kids attend, but not for the poor. There's a lot of evidence that parochial schools educate better than inner-city public schools. If inner-city kids want to go there, I say, "let them. "

JP: Let's have more background: In 1996, Ohio was the first state to grant vouchers that might be used in religious schools.[9] The Wisconsin Supreme Court ruled in favor of them in 1998.[10] In 1999, however, the "Ohio Supreme Court struck down a voucher program that allowed Cleveland children to attend private schools, including church-sponsored schools, at public expense,"[11] and a federal judge in Cleveland blocked a similar program as well.[12] However, the outcry following that decision, by thousands of parents, was so great that the next day he reversed himself.[13] In a sharply-divided opinion, the Supreme Court of the United States allowed the Cleveland voucher program to stand.[14] So, which way? Let the poor people choose, or make them stay until we can improve the public schools?

OF: Better to stay and fight for higher quality.

OF: No, competition by alternative schools is the only way for inner-city schools to get off their [expletive deleted] and improve.

JP: Let's consider the polls. Most Americans initially favored charter schools and vouchers, but over time their enthusiasm has cooled, and they turn more to believing that public schools should be strengthened with whatever budget is available. But this is the public in general. The overwhelming demand by the underprivileged for charter schools or vouchers has convinced me that poor families do care for their children, probably as much as the more privileged, and any thought to the contrary is stereotype.

To summarize, I see two principal issues. The first is whether students and their parents should have choice over their schools. There are many other questions that we haven't considered, such as whether to teach new math or multiplication tables, bilingual education (in English and Spanish or other native languages), American history or other history, and English/American literary classics, or Asian, African, or Latin American writings. Should parents and students choose among schools with different offerings, or should all public schools be alike in a given city, with the curriculum determined by the school board? The second point is whether alternative schools - not ruled by school boards - should be promoted. What do Friends think?

[Minutes taken by the recording clerk show that most participants favored choice and alternative schools but did not know how to bring them about. The question of church versus state was not resolved, and many felt uneasy about "abandoning" the public schools to less motivated students whose parents did not care.]

JP: Here's what I see as the way that might open. All public schools would be contracted out to private bodies, who would determine the curriculum and standards. Parents and students would choose among these schools. Instead of government financing, all students would pay full tuition, from kindergarten through graduate school. Thus the church-vs.-state problem is solved - no public funds at all. A loan fund would be set up, so that *all* students (rich or poor) might borrow for tuition and expenses. They would pay back over their lifetimes, like mortgages, maybe in proportion to their incomes. Any student would be guaranteed admission to some school for which he or she qualifies. The older generation - the ones who had been educated - would replenish the fund for the next generation by paying back its loans.

[The recording clerk noted that the meeting was not in unity. Most OFs thought JP was a wild-eyed optimist who trusted too much in the free market. His plan can never come about, they said, because those with riches or private power would take advantage. JP thought that these OFs, not familiar with history, saw only the *present,* not the *path* we are already taking and where it might lead. He questioned whether Friends credited the poor with the ability to stand up for themselves *even if* the playing field has been leveled. Do Friends still believe in the inner light, he asked, having faith that private individuals can resolve the injustices meted out to the poor and underprivileged?

The recording clerk's final minute was a question: "Did we seek the truth?" Not knowing the answer, the workshop approved only the question.]

NOTES

[1] *New York Times Magazine,* 1/16/00.
[2] *New York Times Magazine,* 1/16/00.
[3] *New York Times,* 11/18/99.
[4] *New York Times,* 8/24/96.
[5] *New York Times,* 1/13/99.
[6] *Wall Street Journal,* 2/12/99.
[7] *New York Times,* 10/26/99.
[8] *Wall Street Journal,* 10/11/96.
[9] *New York Times,* 8/28/96.

[10] *New York Times,* 6/11/98.
[11] *Wall Street Journal,* 5/28/99.
[12] *Wall Street Journal,* 8/25/99.
[13] *New York Times,* 8/28/99.
[14] *New York Times,* 11/6/99.

Chapter 14

"Hey, Hey, Ho, Ho, WTO Has Got to Go - Globalization Too"

Hey, Hey, Ho, Ho, WTO Has Got to Go! So sang the protesters who brought both the WTO (World Trade Organization) and the City of Seattle to a halt in November, 1999. My travels among Friends had ended by that time, so we did not discuss the most controversial issue of the year, if not the decade. Although most of the protests were peaceful, "police in full riot gear with armoured personnel carriers fired tear gas and rubber bullets at protesters who refused to move. Masked youths rampaged through the streets, smashing shop windows."[1]

Suppose the two sides had discussed the controversy in the manner of Friends. In order to imagine this unlikely circumstance, below I have simulated such a conversation, between a protestor designated as "P," whom we assume to be a Friend, and an advocate of the WTO designated as "A." Since both protesters and advocates have tended to be confrontational, the simulation below does not represent their arguments as they actually made them. *Instead, they are the positions that might have been taken had the actors been Friendly and non-confrontational.*

P: We have three principal complaints against the WTO. First, it facilitates the export of jobs from the United States to areas of cheap labor. Second, it forces the United States to weaken environmental protections when other nations, with lower standards, declare such protections to be trade discrimination against them. Third, its negotiations are not transparent. The world outside is affected by what they decide but hears nothing of it until the decisions are made. This is not democratic. [In fact, many more complaints were voiced at Seattle, but these major ones are all we have space for.]

A: Before taking up these questions, let us consider what the WTO is. The WTO is the culmination of seven decades of talks among nations on how to reduce barriers to trade. It is based on the proposition that those nations that trade most are the ones that promote the prosperity of their citizens and bring their people up from poverty.

This proposition has been virtually proven by history. Europe, the United States, and Japan are today's most developed areas. England has had wide open trade for centuries; in continental Europe and Japan internal (within-country) barriers were torn down in the nineteenth century and external barriers reduced in the twentieth. The Asian "tigers" - South Korea, Taiwan, Hong Kong, and Singapore - have grounded their startling advancement in the twentieth century mostly on free trade. The *1999 Index of Economic Freedom* shows that "countries with the most economic freedom also have higher rates of economic growth; their people are better off, at all income levels."[2]

Trade barriers, such as tariffs, quotas, and other restrictions, make goods more costly to consumers. For example, you pay more for your sugar than if you could import it freely from the Dominican Republic, or elsewhere. These extra costs are especially hard on the poor, who spend almost all their income on consumption.

P: You seem to be more concerned about consumers than you are about workers.

A: I'm concerned for workers too. Counterintuitive though it may seem, free trade creates more jobs than it takes away. Textile workers in the United States might lose their jobs if textiles are not protected, but workers in other countries would gain jobs. With their new incomes, they would buy (say) wheat from the United States. The unemployed textile workers would find new jobs making farm machines, or goods for export. Incomes of all are increased if each one is producing the goods for which 'one' is most fit.

The six-decade-long trade talks have already reduced tariffs worldwide to less than half what they were in 1929. This freer trade, which makes it possible for you to buy cars and stereo sets from Japan instead of paying more for them at home, leaves you with more money to spend on other things. It has also created millions of new jobs in the United States. Thus it is one of the causes of the greatest prosperity the United States has seen in its history. The

United States now has the lowest unemployment rates in the world and in history and among the highest wages in the world. That's how workers benefit as well as consumers.

P: That theory is all fine. But it is not felt by the textile workers who lose their jobs. The same for the steel workers, who were in Seattle en masse.

A: It must be very hard on both textile and steel workers to see their jobs, livelihoods, and whole towns decaying. But I didn't promise you a rose garden. The United States should not be producing steel at all. Let's leave that for the less developed countries, that badly need new industry, and we can buy our steel from them. For American steel and textile workers to try to hold their jobs is like trying to stop the tide. The world moves on, and they would do better to move with it.

Inventiveness is in the blood of many people, who think of new ways of producing things. Computers, TVs, cleaner engines, and so on. As these are invented, others must adapt, by losing old jobs and taking new ones. In an inventive society, they can always find jobs. If the new jobs pay less than the old ones, that is only because the job-seeker has not had the proper training. Instead of protecting the textile and steel workers, we must find ways to re-train them and facilitate their moves into expanding industries.

P: I still don't like the idea of multinational corporations moving to other countries to find cheaper labor.

A: We saw in Chapter 9 that this "cheaper labor" is usually a better job than any other that workers in Asia and Africa could find. Some *maquiladora* (border-factory) workers from Mexico were complaining in Seattle about conditions in their factories. "Why don't you take other jobs?" they were asked. "We can't find any," they replied. The foul-smelling *maquiladora* is better than any alternative. Over time, it becomes the road to better conditions as well.

Should a Mexican be pushed out of a job to preserve it for an American? Is a Mexican worker any less a child of God than the American worker? The American can more easily find another job than the Mexican and in the meantime is protected by unemploy-

ment insurance, which the Mexican may not have. The WTO is helping bring jobs where people are poorest, where jobs are most needed.

P: Among the protesters were farmers from South Africa,
who said that subsidized wheat from the United States was ruining
their livelihood.

A: I agree with them. Subsidized agricultural exports are
quite unfair to other countries and hold back farm development there.
Through the WTO, the United States has been trying to persuade
other countries to reduce their farm subsidies in exchange for us
reducing ours. But this is a tough one, since farmers are politically
powerful in Europe and the United States. The South African farmers would do well to direct their protests against Congress and European governments, not against the agency that is trying to help them.

P: Let's turn to the environment. The United States passed
a law requiring fishers for tuna to re-shape their equipment to minimize the number of dolphin caught incidentally. The limit is known
as the dolphin kill rate. Mexico does not have such a law. Since it is
less costly if they don't abide by the maximum kill, Mexicans would
have a competitive advantage over U.S. tuna fishers. So the U.S.
banned tuna from Mexico. Mexico complained, and the WTO found
against the United States, requiring us to suspend the maximum
dolphin kill. That's an example of weakening our environmental
regulations.

A: Not quite true. It did not require us to suspend the maximum dolphin kill, and we did not do so. *The WTO cannot force any
nation to do anything.* All it can do is say that by banning Mexican
tuna the U.S. has violated the rules. Mexico has the right to demand
compensation or to retaliate against U.S. exports. However, what's
good for the goose is good for the gander. If the United States can
ban the import of Mexican tuna, Mexico should have the right to
ban U.S. products. (But trade wars tend to escalate. They are never
productive in the long run.)

In fact, the U.S. and Mexico have begun negotiations on
how the Mexicans can reduce their dolphin kill, and they have not
retaliated. Mexicans don't like to be called dolphin-killers, but reducing the kill rate is not an easy political matter for them, espe-

cially when they feel the U.S. is dictating their policies. We reach consensus slowly. You Quakers should understand that.

Another case would be that of Mexican trucks. "Citing safety concerns, the Clinton administration has decided to delay opening all 50 states to Mexican trucks and buses . . . , as is called for by the North American Free Trade Agreement. Mexican officials denounced the decision as a violation of the 1993 trade pact, which calls for letting Mexican trucks and buses travel anywhere north of the border beginning on Jan. 1, 2000."[3] This could be a case for the WTO, to decide whether the United States is banning Mexican trucks to preserve the environment or to create an advantage for American truckers. If the WTO decides against the United States, we still don't have to admit Mexican trucks, but Mexico would have the right to ban our products in retaliation, or demand a penalty payment, or better yet, negotiate. The negotiations might well lead to greater Mexican controls over their trucks' pollution. The WTO would be an impartial agency for conducting those negotiations.

These cases raise two much broader questions: Should we, the United States, ban imports from any country that does not meet our environmental standards? If so, we might end up banning trade from most of the world. If we set our own environmental standards by sovereign right, should not other countries have the same privilege?

Let's return to the basic purpose of the WTO, which is to bring about nondiscrimination among producers all over the world. Over time it is negotiating away the tariffs, quotas, and other bans that favor producers in one country over another. But it is an explicit principle of the WTO that environmental protections remain within the sovereignty of each country. Thus the Americans and Mexicans are each sovereign over the maximum dolphin kill, or clean air regulations, or pollution by trucks, or other environmental protections within their respective territories.

So we have a dilemma. High environmental standards are costly, and less developed countries (LDCs) often cannot afford them. Not only can more developed countries (MDCs) better afford environmental standards, but they are the ones who want them most.

One economic study shows that countries with per capita income of $5,000 are on the threshold of demanding environmental protections. As per capita income grows well above $5,000, the more they want protections.[4] That is why Europe and the United States demand greater environmental protection than Mexico, for instance. Other studies show that trade is historically a strong factor in increasing per capita incomes in LDCs. So if we cut off trade from LDCs, we diminish the probability that they will become MDCs and improve their environmental protections.

P: So, what does WTO see as the answer?

A: Let me summarize. Environmental regulations being a sovereign matter, any country may set whatever standards it wishes. But it violates the WTO agreements if it bans imports from a country that does not meet its standards. The WTO cannot stop it from banning imports, however. Therefore, because the importing country violates the WTO finding, it should pay compensation to the exporting country, or else that country has the right to retaliate. For example, Mexico could ban the import of American wheat (but has not found it politically expedient to do so).

P: I don't think many protesters will agree with all that. Many protestors think that the WTO is forcing the United States to lower its environmental standards.

A: We have already seen that this is not true. The WTO cannot force the United States to do anything. All it can do is give the other country the right to retaliate.

On your next question, I agree with you that negotiations by the WTO ought to be more transparent. Not only will the outside world know what the WTO is doing, but they will see that it is often not really doing what they think it is doing. The sessions might be broadcast on TV, for example. So should those of the United Nations, the International Monetary Fund, and the World Bank. Congress, too. If the protesters had marched outside the meeting place waving their banners but still let the ministers in, then the ministers might have seen the need to tell the outside world what they were doing. However, the protesters barred their entry, so they didn't have that chance. I question whether preventing the ministers from entering the WTO meetings is the most effective way to bring about greater transparency.

Now, I have two questions for you. First, I know that many Quakers protested in Seattle. A recent cover of *The Economist*[5] shows a pitiful Indian child, wrapped in a shabby cloak, with a heart-rending look in her eyes. The article, "The Real Losers [from Seattle]," tells her story: "Above all, she needs education, and health, and much else. But without trade, and the faster growth it can bring, she is unlikely to get any of it." Do you Quakers know that economists the world over believe this statement is correct?

Second, Quakers have long favored international negotiations. You have conducted programs to bring diplomats together to talk informally. You were among those cheering the United Nations when it was founded, and you have a Quaker U.N. office in New York. Along comes another organization, this time the WTO, also based on internationalism and negotiation, this time to work out the rules of international trade. And many of you rise up in protest. Why the change?

P: I hear your arguments, but many protesters won't agree with them.

A: Fine. It is not the purpose of this book to persuade anyone. Rather, it aims to open up both sides to Friendly debate instead of confrontation. If I seem to favor one side, that's just because I do. Don't think of which position I take, or which you take. Rather, let's encourage readers to continue the discussion among yourselves and seek the truth in the various positions. I would, however, like to close with a word from our author.

JP: Decades ago, the Young Friends of New York (to which I belonged) favored world government. Like many others, I joined the Student Federalists. Since then, I have stepped back, realizing that a world government of powers that have not yet learned democracy will not work. But trade is a small segment of world cooperation, and let us start with a small segment. Over decades I watched the slow negotiations, from the highest tariff in our nation's history in 1929, through the reciprocal trade agreements of the thirties, then the GATT (General Agreement on Tariffs and Trade) after World War II, and finally the WTO. Each time I cheered on the move toward multilateralism, globalization, and nondiscrimination among nations.

For Quakers, the task ahead is to know peoples of different cultures, not to hinder investment in them or trade with them. Let us help them set up universal environmental standards, to which we may all subscribe. Let us also help them improve the productivity of labor so their workers will earn wages similar to those in our country. Let us use multinational agencies like the United Nations and the WTO to achieve our goals alongside other nations.

I admire the NGOs (nongovernment organizations), which were far better organized in Seattle and had built more coalitions than the delegates to the WTO. I long to see many aspects of democracy transferred from legislative halls to NGOs. But the NGOs need to wander more through the slums in Asia, Africa, and Latin America (as I have) and visit factories there (as I have). They need to talk more with the poorest of the poor, whom they purport to advocate. They also need to study more economics, to understand how their proposals - most of them far more complex than they think - often end up with the opposite effects of those intended.

I wept to see "my baby" trashed in Seattle by those who should have nurtured it. After all, they share my goal to pull the world out of poverty and make us equals.

NOTES

[1] *The Economist,* 12/4/99.
[2] Published by the Heritage Foundation and *The Wall Street Journal.* Quotation is from *The Wall Street Journal,* 11/30/99.
[3] *New York Times,* 1/8/00.
[4] G. Grossman and A. Krueger, "Environmental Impacts of a North American Free Trade Area Agreement," in P. Garber, ed., *The Mexico-U.S. Free Trade Agreement,* Cambridge, MA, MIT Press, 1993.
[5] December 11-17, 1999.

Chapter 15

"Capitalists are Greedy for Profits"

As Robin and I drove home through Nebraska after a tour of eastern Quakers, she was struck by the rich green fields (I was busy watching the road). "I haven't seen many cows," she remarked.

"Right here," I replied, "with fertile soil and rainfall, farmers can make more on corn and soybeans. Eastern Colorado and Texas have more cattle, because the land is drier, more adapted to extensive grasses. Western ranches couldn't make money if they tried to grow green crops.

In the workshops from which we were returning, many Friends had been negative about profits. To some, profits indicated greed. Others had said they preferred not to live in an economy based on profit. Still others would seek to create more nonprofit agencies.

I believe the movie, "Pirates of Silicon Valley," on how Steve Jobs and Bill Gates got started in computers, reflects what Friends were saying. This movie accurately depicts a dog-eat-dog attitude of greed and power, and illegal methods or those of doubtful legality, to dominate the computer market, then the Internet. Secrets are stolen and copyrights violated, with slight changes to make the software legal. Microsoft has used its market power to demand that computer manufacturers load its own software instead of competing brands. I join Friends who do not want the world they live in to be like that.

Yet there is a legitimate role for profit. The profit motive assumes that, when given a choice between two identical products, one costing more, the other less, most buyers will choose the cheaper product. The producer knows this, so 'one' either tries to produce at lowest cost, to have the low-price product, or else to add value to the product so that more people are willing to pay the 'little extra.' If we do not live in a competitive economy, how would we persuade producers to lower prices or produce better products?

The cornfields of Nebraska are an example. To maximize profits, different foods are grown where the climate and soil are best for each. This brings the greatest food production on given land and resources. Even in manufacturing, producers generally have strong incentives to use the best tools and machines for their purposes, hire the amount of labor necessary with the right skills, and out come the most goods and services with available resources.

This, of course, is the theory. Reality differs in many ways. Some producers (farm or manufacturing) make the wrong guesses on kinds of product and labor, some use more resources than they need because they do not manage well. For the most part, these firms are driven out of business by more efficient competitors. Largely because production seeks the greatest profit, the United States produces the most with the least waste of resources and therefore is today the wealthiest nation in the world. Furthermore, that production - and the jobs that go with it - create greater employment and greater incomes, even for the poor, than in any other country.

As a Quaker, I have admired simplicity and detested not only greed and business piracy, but more: lavish displays of consumer goods at Christmas. What a dilemma! How could I reconcile the legitimate role of profit with the piracy of Silicon Valley, obnoxious advertising, and excessive consumerism?

To reconcile this conflict, I came to feel that greed and ostentatious display are *personal* characteristics, not *systemic* ones. It is possible to resist the most charismatic advertising. Long ago my family - at the initiative of our children - gave up buying Christmas presents for all. We drew lots, and each person gave and received only one present. The children, home from school for vacation, said they would rather spend time with each other than out shopping. A few Christmases later, we gave up even the one bought present and decided to give only what we had ourselves made.

Not all businesspeople are greedy, and it is not Friendly to stereotype them. Many businesses are conducted without the viciousness of the pirates of Silicon Valley. When you compare prices in the grocery store, seeking the lowest for the same quality, are you greedy, trying to maximize the profit of the family? I don't think so;

instead, you are keeping the supermarkets in line. So also do businesspeople keep their competitors in line.

Even if the capitalist system does promote greed, so does every other system in which goods are produced - feudal, religious, socialist, communist, military, dictatorship, or what have you. For many years, socialists "persuaded" us that their system worked without greed - until we discovered that socialism concentrated power over people, caused great waste in resources (because it was not based on profit), and caused hunger and hardship for the poor. That is why the Soviet Union collapsed. Greed or generosity, and simple or complex living, depend on the character of the individual, not the kind of productive system. These qualities are nurtured in our families, churches, and schools, and by peer-group pressures.

Friends were not always convinced by this plea. Doesn't making profits mean you fire workers? Shouldn't we be more forgiving of companies that are not managed well? Give them more time?

I have great sympathy with these questions. However, in our rapid-change economy, I replied to Friends, capital, management, and workers all have to move from one activity to another as both products and ways of making them change. Unprofitable firms have to be driven out of business, and their managers must learn from their mistakes. Workers must learn new skills and find new jobs.

These are harsh facts. I have a friend whose husband worked for two firms that both went bankrupt. On one occasion they had just had a baby, and on another their oldest child was eight. I wish I could have helped them. Here, I believe we should take a lesson from the hurricanes that periodically batter the East coast and other parts. We do not build stronger walls to stop them because we cannot. Instead, we do all we can to minimize the suffering, first moving the inhabitants out of harm's way and then helping them rebuild.

Stopping economic change is like stopping the hurricane. Instead of complaining about things we can't change, Friends would do well to seek ways to make the transition easy, like unemployment insurance, helping new industries form, or retraining workers.

Friends were still not always convinced. To many of them, profits still meant dollars for advertising, to persuade consumers to buy goods they didn't need. Greed and lavish displays are both contrary to the simple way of life to which Friends aspire. How would they reconcile these principles with the plea that only profit causes the right goods and services to be produced with the least waste?

The answer - I believe - is by accepting that greed and consumerism are personal characteristics, to be overcome by personal discipline. Furthermore, though profit is the prime motivator in business, businesspeople do have others as well. They may want to produce the best mousetrap possible, no matter what they earn. I started my career in business (as a CPA) and have also served in government. Had I stayed with either, my net worth would be considerably greater than it is now. But I preferred the life of a teacher, because of the joy of inter-acting with students and writing books. (My royalties have always been a pittance.) Do I have any right to say that others are not similarly motivated in whatever careers they choose?

Many times during my 1999 tour did the name of Bill Gates come up. "Why should he have so many billions," Friends asked, "when there are so many poor around the world?"

That was a tough one. We all know why he *does* have his billions. The question was: why *should* he? More to the point, what are the alternatives? Would you take it away from him in taxes? (That might both make the government too powerful and reduce Bill's incentive to improve Windows). Would you require him to pay more in wages? (His employees are already overpaid compared to other industries.) Should he distribute it evenly over the world's poor? (Each one would get a few pennies). Should he spend more on his personal consumption, to pass the money on to others? (Friends were aghast at that idea; he is already a conspicuous consumer, with that big house of his.) So, what will he do with so much money that he can't "take with him."

Few Friends asked what he *is* doing with it. I understand - this is rumor only, but from informed sources - that he has decided to leave each of his kids no more than a million dollars so they will not grow up to be no-good bums. (Some Friends thought even that was excessive.) The only thing left for him is to put it into foundations - he is one of the biggest contributors to research on AIDS and other diseases. In 1999, he pledged $1 billion for scholarships for minority students "in the field of education, math, science, and engineering, . . . promising them enough money to cover tuition, room and board, and other expenses through college and any graduate degrees they pursue."[1] If you do not believe he should have had that money in the first place, do you then also say that those minority students should not have the scholarships?

Bill Gates is just one billionaire. What has happened to wealth accumulated by others - by the "robber barons" of the nineteenth century, for example? Or by the great trading companies of the seventeenth and eighteenth centuries? Do wealthy dynasties go on for generation after generation? Strange, no Friends asked these questions; I had to bring them up myself.

The answer: They used to, but for the most part, not any more. The dynasties of feudal times were based more on land, nobility, and royalty. Laws, especially primogeniture (that Jane Austen wrote about), helped the rich keep their wealth in the family, not dissipate it. Present-day laws, especially the inheritance tax, work the other way around. Besides, estates are harder to keep intact in a world economy founded more on capital than on land.

Oh yes, the Rockefellers and the Mellons are probably still rich, but as time goes on such wealth becomes dissipated. David Landes, Harvard historian, has a rule of "rags to riches to rags in three generations." (Sometimes it takes a bit longer). The first generation invents, the second manages well, and the third becomes spendthrifts.

What about monopolies? Suppose a market has only one producer and no substitute, or more likely a dominant producer so the products of others are not true substitutes. I wanted to find an alternative to my Iomega backup drive, but I was dismayed to find no other product of equal quality or price. "Equal quality or price" - that is the key. No law, no rare material, no scarcity of labor prevents other companies from competing with Iomega. It has reached the pinnacle of the product because it produces the best at the lowest price. If it were to raise its price, or lower the quality of its product, others would start to compete. To my thinking, Iomega would be a monopoly only if no other producer *could* enter the market, not just if none *did.*

How many companies are there in this globalized world that are true monopolies, for example by owning the entire world supply of a given resource, in the sense that no other company can compete with them? Only those protected by patents. But if we abolish patents we won't know how to reward inventors. Our answer has been a compromise: to award patents, but to limit their life.

Competition and free selection of technology and quality of product are not available in any economy other than one of profit-making enterprise. Furthermore, a free-enterprise economy allows the greatest scope for initiative, innovation, and invention, human qualities that are largely suppressed in directed economies, such as a socialist one. This is probably why the United States economy has the highest productivity in the world, among the highest wages, and (until recent years) the most equitable distribution of income. (See Chapter 3 to find out what became of that!)

What, then, about the pirates of Silicon Valley? As an economic historian, I have "seen" the piracy of other generations: city fathers of the Middle Ages who destroyed the roads of other cities so traders would not go to them; port cities that silted the harbors of other cities for the same reason; trading companies of the seventeenth century whose ships traveled armed and made war on each other; slave capturers of the eighteenth century; and the robber barons of the nineteenth. But I have also seen how Westerners and Japanese figured out ways to overcome these monstrosities,[2] and I have no doubt that the same will happen to the pirates of Silicon Valley. If one takes the long view, over centuries, present-day practices become no more obnoxious than earlier, and no more difficult to overcome.

Nevertheless I believe the distribution of income and wealth is still more concentrated than it should be in both the United States and the world. I believe many people are more greedy than Friends would like. I believe many are more consumption-minded than is desirable. But all these are moral shortcomings, to be overcome at the personal level. Abolishing profit is not the way.

Unfortunately, if we *think* greed and ostentatious display are promoted by the system, and if we stereotype all business people as greedy, then we spend our time trying to change the system instead of trying to understand and improve the people. This, I believe, is one of the principal shortcomings of Quaker thinking today.

When Robin and I stopped for the night with friends in Kearny, Nebraska, we tasted fresh-picked corn - it was so cheap, yet so delicious. I hope the farmer made a profit.

NOTES

[1] *New York Times,* 0/16/99.
[2] I have written about this history in *Centuries of Economic Endeavor.*

Chapter 16

"Great Disparities between CEO Pay and Ordinary Workers"

Salaries of corporate executive officers (CEOs) have increased enormously, relative to those of ordinary workers. As of January 1999, the average CEO in a selection of companies chosen by unions (therefore, the highest group) took home $7.8 million, or 326 times the pay of the average worker. This compares with a ratio of 44:1 in the 1960s.[1]

Friends in my summer workshops were aghast. So am I. Most thought that if the company could afford to give the CEO such high pay, it should instead pay it to the workers. As economic historian, however, I had a few questions. How long has this been going on? Has it ever happened before? If it has happened, why, and how long did the disparities last? What caused them to end, if they did? How long are they likely to last now?

The answers: Today's disparities have been building up for about twenty years. Yes, they have happened before. One such time was during the industrial revolution of the eighteenth century, when enclosures forced English farmers off the land and into urban factories, with dismal conditions and very low pay. These conditions lasted almost a century, but they improved after that. Why did they improve? The growth of industry and a scarcity of labor opened new opportunities for workers. Population in the nineteenth century did not grow as rapidly as Parson Malthus had predicted, and workers could demand higher pay. Do we want to wait another hundred years for the same to happen now? Most Friends I know don't. Neither do I. So, what can we do about it?

Before answering that, we must know more about why and how the disparities came about. There are two mechanisms by which CEO pay has increased.

Stock Options

The first consists of stock options, which are pieces of paper that the CEO (or other high-ranking officer) receives as part of 'one's' salary, which 'one' may exchange for company stock, usually at the current market price. If the market price rises, the officer will gain by saving the options for a later date. In the meantime, 'one' will have taken no risk, because 'one' did not pay for them in the first place. Presumably this system gives the CEO more incentive to manage the business well, so its profits will increase, driving up the stock price. "Stock-option grants accounted for a record 53.3% of the compensation given by America's top companies in 1998 to their chief executives. This compares with 26% in 1994 and a mere 2% in the mid-1980s."[2]

However, many CEOs - possibly almost all - do not cash in their options or sell their stock. Until they do, they can't use the money for buying luxury houses. In fact, many companies require their high-ranking officers to hold stock so long as they are employed. If they are not cashed or sold, these stocks or options are mere pieces of paper, doing the CEO no good at all except to make 'one' feel richer (on paper). They leave just as many goods available to others as if they had not been issued. This condition can go on for years.

Many Friends would like to see the options paid to workers instead of to CEOs. So would I, except for two problems. For one, workers would be more likely than CEOs to cash in their options and sell their stocks. This would mean many sellers and few buyers. Trying to find scarce buyers, sellers would drastically lower the stock offer prices; others would panic and sell stocks they were holding. All this might cause a market crash, leading into another depression like that of the 1930s. For the other, wages in high-earning companies would rise much out of line with those of workers in small, family enterprises. Small enterprises (of less than 500 employees) generate 80% of American employment and 76% of salary incomes.[3] Many are not stock companies at all. Employees of government and nonprofits would also be excluded. Instead of an elite of CEOs, we would create a small elite of high-paid workers in choice companies like Microsoft.

Cash Pay

The second mechanism is cash pay. CEOs also receive higher salaries in cash, presumably because of their value to corporations in building profits. CEOs must oversee very complex organizations, making sure that all the pieces fit precisely and skilled midlevel managers make the correct decisions. They must make educated guesses on the future of the economy and know what their competitors are doing. We are now in a period of rapidly changing management practices, where the skills of a CEO perceptive enough to foresee where the company is moving are scarcer, relative to demand, than they have been for at least two centuries.

It is hard enough to find a CEO with all the necessary management skills if one were standing on a stationary platform. Now consider a moving one: the technological revolution has brought about vast changes in management practices, so that all the qualities of a skilled manager are constantly required in new forms.

Boards of directors make mistakes, often choosing CEOs that lack the requisite qualities. Some observers believe they do this for cronyism. I doubt that cronyism is a prime cause, since boards that appoint inexperienced cronies spell disaster for the firm. Rather, I think boards have a hard time knowing who is a good manager in rapidly changing circumstances.

One thing is certain: Experienced CEOs demand high pay. Since the number of qualified CEOs is less than the number of corporations needing them, they accept offers from the highest bidders. If this is unjust, the only answer is to increase the supply of qualified CEOs, to bring down their price. How? First, break the glass ceiling, to admit the many qualified women to CEO ranks. Second, train more managers in the nation's business schools. Third, seek and identify more qualified persons. But obstacles loom before all these. Breaking the glass ceiling requires demolishing long-held prejudices. The mere possession of an MBA does not supply the requisite experience. Identifying the indispensable skills also requires experience; it is no lottery.

On the other side of employment, the capabilities of workers also need improvement, so they can demand higher pay. But that requires fundamental changes in our education system. (See Chapter 13).

Increasing the numbers of innovative managers and improving the skills of workers are the only true answers. Anything less than that will lead to disappointment.

How long will all this take? My guess - a sheer one - is only forty years, if we start now. Our economy is moving much more rapidly than that of eighteenth-century England. But if we do something wrong now - like decreeing higher pay for workers and lower pay for CEOs by government mandate - we will set up such social dissension, and such industrial inefficiency, that the truth might take one hundred years to find instead of forty.

[The recording clerk noted that workshop participants and I were in unity that the gap was too large, but some participants thought it might be narrowed by government direct action. Thinking it is too difficult to beat the market, I thought instead that the gap would narrow only if the supply of competent CEOs were increased and the skills of workers were upgraded. Though not in unity on that point, we had sought the truth together.]

NOTES

[1] *The Economist,* 1/30/99.
[2] *The Economist,* 8/7/99:18.
[3] Calculated from *Statistical Abstract of the United States, 1998*: table 866, p. 547.

Chapter 17

"The Economy is Dominated by Corporations"

In my summer workshops I met Friends who felt that multinational corporations dominated the world economy. Many had heard how United Fruit Company had fomented a revolution in Guatemala or how International Telephone and Telegraph (ITT) had tried to instigate one in Chile or how del Monte had tried to usurp land in the Philippines. Since I had done professional assignments in all three of these countries, I knew they had a point. I lived in the Philippines shortly after the del Monte scandal, and although I did not have first-hand knowledge, I know that many Filipinos believed it to be true.

At about the time of the ITT scandal, I had to go to Chile to lecture in the university in Santiago. Before leaving, I called on Harold Geneen, President of ITT, in New York, to hear his opinion. He did not tell me that ITT was plotting to overthrow the government, but he did say that he greatly feared that his company would be nationalized, as American copper companies had been, and that stockholders in the United States would lose their investments.

The "ITT Papers," leaked from inside memos by an ITT employee, told how ITT and the CIA were plotting with the Chilean military for a coup in case the socialist Salvador Allende were elected President. The papers were not circulated in the United States, but I was in Santiago shortly after the scandal broke, and I bought a copy in the streets. Wondering whether they were true or not, I later visited the Undersecretary of State for Latin American Affairs in Washington, who was a personal friend. He said they were true, and he was furious that all this had happened behind his back. He had not been notified, because it was known that he would oppose it.

I have also visited Guatemala several times and found that government officials there all say the U.S. intervention took place, but they were divided on whether it was caused by United Fruit Company or whether the communist government was overthrown because it was stockpiling munitions from the Soviet Union, thus constituting a danger to all Central American states.

Friends in my workshops also cited how American corporations are spreading themselves all over the world, taking employment away from the United States. Some of those corporations have annual incomes higher than the revenues of the governments in the countries where they serve. How could they help but dominate the government?

But there is another side to the story, of LDC (less developed country) governments dominating the corporations. I do not justify governments dominating corporations or corporations dominating government. I favor an even playing field. The following examples are intended only offset the widely-held belief that multinational corporations alone have the advantage.

One day when I was economic advisor to Philip Ndegwa, the Permanent Secretary of Finance in Kenya - his office was counterpart to that of Secretary of the Treasury in the United States - Philip had invited representatives of all the major oil companies wanting to do business in Kenya (about fifteen) to come to the Ministry of Finance to hear the terms. Philip and I represented Kenya; his was the only black face at the table. He laid down the terms, which were not what the corporation officials had hoped to hear. At the end, he got up and walked out of the room, leaving me to take their questions. "Does he really mean it?" they all wanted to know, perhaps thinking that because I had a white face I would be on their side. "He really means it," I replied.

Here is another case, this time the government of Venezuela standing up to the oil companies. The Articles of Agreement of the International Monetary Fund require that member governments supply the Fund with their annual balance of payments statements. In 1950, when I was a fresh PhD working for the Fund, Venezuela had not complied, because the foreign oil companies refused to hand over their information to the central bank. A balance of payments statement without oil would make no sense for Venezuela. The Fund sent me to Caracas to see what I could do.

I visited the comptrollers of the major oil companies. They would not give the data directly to the central bank because they feared that the government might use the information against them.

But they would give the data to me, provided I would consolidate the statements of all the oil companies and give only consolidated information to the central bank, keeping the individual data as their secret and mine. The fact that I was a CPA and had worked with Price Waterhouse, a very large accounting firm, persuaded them. CPAs are expected to keep company data confidential. All this I did, and the first balance of payments statement of Venezuela was published.

Two years later, the Government of Venezuela required by law that the companies supply the data to the central bank, and they did. Later, all the major oil companies all over the world were expropriated and turned into state companies, Venezuelan among them. Still later, most governments, including Venezuela, discovered they did not have the expertise to run oil companies, so they invited the majors back, sometimes as consultants to the state oil companies, sometimes as independent companies, and sometimes as partners. Clearly, however, the government was in charge.

Here is still another case, this time the government of Peru dominating the oil companies: When the new military government of Peru expropriated Esso in 1968, I visited the Undersecretary of State for Latin America (a different one this time) in Washington to find out what the U.S. response would be. He said the United States could no longer stop expropriations of multinational corporations in sovereign countries; all it would do would be to urge that compensation be made based on fair value of the company assets.

Still another case, this time the government of Mexico bringing the oil companies to heel. Just before World War II, Mexico nationalized American oil companies. Their chief executive officers urged President Roosevelt to intervene. Roosevelt refused, not because of morality but probably because he needed Mexico on our side in the impending war. He said the oil companies should do their own negotiations. The companies were nationalized, but the parent companies sailed away with all their ships, so that the new Mexican company - Petroleos Mexicanos, or Pemex - could not export. But Pemex supplied its oil mostly to Mexico, initiating the profound economic development that has taken place there since then.

As I mulled over the Friends' objections to multinationals taking jobs away from Americans, I thought back on how - every time I had a foreign assignment - I would wander through the slums of the country I was visiting. I have visited the slums of all Latin American countries except Cuba and many African countries. In Cali, Colombia, I stumbled upon a land invasion, where 16,000 homeless persons had set up illegal shacks. When the army came to burn their shacks and arrest their leaders, an American friend and I secreted one of the leaders in a Volkswagen and covered him with a blanket as he crouched between the front and back seats. I put my feet on top of him, as if I were just lounging in the back seat. The soldiers did not see him as we drove him through their lines to safety.[1]

I would talk to slumdwellers at random, as well as the land invaders of Cali, asking them questions about jobs, politics, homelessness, or the United States. Most of them were unemployed, their children ill-fed, and they would give anything to find a job. Most felt no rancor toward my country. If a multinational corporation were to take a job from the United States - where workers are well fed, have unemployment insurance, and can find another job - and give it to one of these poor souls, would that be bad? Do not Friends consider that there is that of God in all persons, not just American workers?

According to U.S. law, bribes by American corporations to foreign governments are illegal. For several years, the United States has been urging European countries to join in this ban. In 1998, it extracted such an agreement. Since the culture of less developed countries is one of bribery as a daily routine - indulged in by local companies as well as multinationals - I do not know how well this treaty will be enforced. Multinational corporations complain that the law puts them at a competitive disadvantage with local corporations that pay bribes all the time. The U.S. government has compiled a list of 100 occasions in a single year in which American multinationals lost contracts because they abided by the law.

Therefore, my experience has led me to believe that there is a mixed story. A few multinationals have tried to dominate governments, but for the most part they have failed in the long run, and the long run is now.

Stereotypes

In my sojourns among Friends, I did not meet any racists or religionists. A racist usually stereotypes persons of a different race, assigning them qualities as a group, usually undesirable ones, and often using derogatory terms to describe them. A religionist does the same for members of a different religion. Racists will say, "Niggers do this" or "Niggers do that." Religionists will say, "Jews do this" or "Jews do that." Often they attribute the behavior of a few examples to the collectivity. Usually racists have not studied the races as anthropologists do, nor have religionists treated religions as theologians do. Therefore their stereotypes are based on ignorance.

But I did meet many, many corporationists. A corporationist will say, "Corporations do this" or "Corporations do that." They were not sparing in their invectives, some of which I would not repeat in polite company. Virtually all the corporationists I met had not studied corporations in business school, nor worked in them, nor knew how much they were earning in profits (which they believed were enormous, far greater than they really are), nor how much they paid their workers, nor what benefits they provided. According to a finding by the International Labor Office in 1976, multinational corporations were paying workers in less developed countries on average 100% more than the workers' alternative earning power, and they provided more schools, housing, and health care than their workers would otherwise receive.[2] Above all, they brought technology that the Third World could not get in any other way, thus vastly contributing to overcoming poverty. Nor had any of that changed by January 2000, when *The Economist* reported that in both more and less developed countries, multinational corporations pay higher wages, create jobs faster, and conduct more research than do domestic corporations. For example, foreign firms' wages in Turkey "are 124% above average; their workforce has risen by 11.5% a year compared with 0.6% in domestic ones; and their R&D spending is twice as high as in domestic firms."[3]

Fortunately, not all Friends are corporationists. I suspect that my workshops, by their very titles, attracted a larger proportion of corporationists than are representative of the Society of Friends as a whole.

Stereotyping is for Friends what other religions might call a "sin:" it is behavior contrary to our foundational principles. These principles are (1) that we are always seekers of the truth, and (2) we are open to listening to that of God within others. Seekers of the truth would be open to questions like: how many corporations do this, how many do not, what corporations are "good citizens" and what seems to make that occur? In fact, corporations do not behave as a monolith; they live in a fluid society. In the course of a decade, we can see various sectors assuming market leadership - automobiles - only to be replaced by other sectors - computers. A few markets are deficient in pluralism - Microsoft in computers, for example. But over time, Microsoft will be put in its corporate place by competitors that are already hot on its tail.

The most disconcerting part was that corporationists did not recognize that corporations are made up of people, just the way racists and religionists do not recognize that their targets are "real people." My son, Larry, graduated from college with a major in computer science and was immediately hired by Microsoft. He was on one of the teams that wrote an early version of Windows. After that, he worked on other teams until he decided, at age 32, that he had other values in mind. Among Friends groups, I heard some derogatory remarks about "Microsoft millionaires," so I had to defend Larry and his wife, Wallis, who is also retired from Microsoft. They are engaged in many civic activities. Wallis writes articles in a local paper promoting environmentalism. Larry teaches computers to underprivileged pupils in public schools. He has also written programs for *Acción Internacional,* to promote small-scale loans to rural women in less developed countries. Larry and Wallis together have financed a half-way house in Seattle for women in need of help. I am proud of them.

I sent all my children letters about my traveling under concern among Friends. When she saw my line on corporationists, Wallis replied:

> I'm stopped in my tracks by this insight. We have a friend, familiar with the source of our wealth, who is full of invective concerning multinational corporations, Microsoft, Bill Gates, et cetera. Whilst he professes to be our friend, he despises us. Given the intensity of his hatred for what we represent, I find myself not inclined to spend time in his company. In Seattle, when one moves outside the Microsoft social circle, the venom directed toward the Microsoft millionaire . . . does very much resemble what you have described. We are responsible for the decline of the neighborhood, the degradation of the environment, the sorry state of our public schools, housing beyond reach of the middle class, the decline of civic life, et cetera et cetera. We are boorish, have no manners, do not participate. Even when people know for whom you have worked, they are quite comfortable telling you Bill G. is the Anti-Christ and you his acolyte. I do not think we will ever free ourselves of this tendency to divide and hate one another.

When stereotyping is pointed out, "good people" sometimes artificially differentiate persons from their behavior, as in the case of Larry's and Wallis's friend. The common distinction is to say that one does not despise people in corporations, one only despises what they do. The conversation continues as before, but now with the "good excuse" that we are talking only about behaviors. This would be reprehensible if the object of conversation were a Black person, a poor person, or a woman, but somehow it seemed to be permissible if the object is the CEO of a corporation.

Decades ago, I was on the faculty of high school institutes in international affairs, run by the American Friends Service Committee. Many of the attendees were not Friends, and we Friends appealed to them to give up their hate for other races and other religions. I never thought I would have to appeal to Friends to give up their hate for other people. But for those corporationist Friends, that is what I am doing now.

NOTES

[1] This experience is described in my article, "The Land Grabbers of Cali," *The Reporter,* January 1964.
[2] International Labour Office, Wages and Working Conditions in Multinational Enterprises, Geneva, 1976.
[3] *The Economist,* 1/8/00.

Chapter 18

"Trust Government More than Corporations"

At the end of a workshop in one Yearly Meeting, the leader (not me) asked us to list the lessons learned over the past two days. A long list appeared on the blackboard, one of which was the simple statement: "Trust Government More than Corporations."

Why trust Government? Friends of the seventeenth century scarcely trusted a government that put them in jail and deprived them of their civil and religious rights. Mostly, they were tradespeople, who created a commerce based on trust. It was said that a family could send its children to a Quaker merchant because it knew they would not be cheated. So, Quaker businesses were trusted more than government. Have we reversed roles over the centuries? If so, Why?

I was the only one in that workshop who did not agree to that statement, though after talking with many Friends, I discovered it was far from a universal Quaker position.

Government regulation is necessary to prevent pollution of water and air, to keep drivers on the proper side of the road, to make sure that food is healthy and products identified by their contents, to discourage burglars, and for many other reasons. Why would anyone oppose regulation?

Most Friends to whom I put that question answered, "Profits." That is surely one reason. Economists have long recognized Garret Hardin's "tragedy of the commons," which arose out of the medieval practice of allowing any villager to graze 'one's' cattle on the village commons, which became overgrazed. The same condition applies today to land, forest, air, and water, which may be "owned" by "no one" (except in Colorado, and possibly other states, where every drop of water that comes from rain or mountain streams is owned by someone). Resources available free will be over-used. (See Chapter 5.)

.   Government sometimes responds to environmentalists, who would conserve resources through regulation, but it also represents those who would grab "free" resources and over-use them. Since these "grabbers" are often more politically powerful than environ-mentalists, or can deliver more votes, we should be wary of always trusting government. My solution, proposed in *The Moral Economy,* would be to assign air, water, forests, and public land to nongovern-mental agencies that would be required by their charters to use them well and would be monitored by other nongovernmental agencies to prevent abuse.

This solution conforms to the proposition in *The Moral Economy* that decentralized power has historically brought about prosperity with justice more frequently than has central government, be it king, emperor, shogun, tribal chief, or democracy.[1] The use of nongovernmental agencies parallels our system of checks and bal-ances. Do not put all power over the environment in the hands of the government, since collusion by two parties - government and indus-try - is more likely than collusion among three - government, indus-try, and nongovernmental agencies. But my proposal - if it ever comes at all - is a long way off.

There is, however, another reason why some oppose regula-tion. In *The Moral Economy,* I have proposed a rule that *power ex-pands until other power stops it.* This rule applies to nations, armies, CEOs of corporations, and especially dictatorial governments. But it also applies to regulatory agencies. Once set up, regulatory agencies and courts frequently co-opt more power than Congress and the people had initially intended.

In one case the Supreme Court ruled that farm programs could legally penalize an Ohio farmer for eating flour made from the wheat he had sowed" (because he would be sowing more than the law allowed).[2] In another case, "Garberville, California, residents were threatened with $1,000 fines and a year in prison for hiking on their own property in violation of a government order cordoning off large areas of land being searched for drugs by the military"[3] While laws protecting wetlands are laudatory, in one case housing "devel-opments in the midst of cactus and parched earth [were] classified as 'wetlands' because standing water could occur for 7 days in a hole dug for a foundation"[4]

The Family and Medical Leave Act of 1993 requires employers to give twelve weeks of unpaid leave to new parents. "That sounds good, but its pernicious effect is to dissuade employers from hiring women younger than menopause, or to drive out of business employers who could not afford the cost of locating temporary replacement help or of hiring and training less experienced workers."[5] My favorite case for absurdity is that of a Kansas City bank being ordered to put a "Braille keypad on a drive-through cash machine" presumably for blind customers who drive automobiles. The cases go on and on and on.

An article in the June, 1999, *Readers' Digest,*[6] argues - with citations of reliable authorities - that the Environmental Protection Agency has gone far beyond scientific evidence to pass regulations that are costly but do little or no good. One such case was sent to me by Steve Williams, a Quaker friend: "The Environmental Protection Agency tried to compel a private party to spend $9.3 million on additional cleanup of a waste site, so that children could eat its dirt without ill effect not merely for 70 days a year - the level the party, amazingly, agreed to achieve - but for 245 days a year."[7] If we allow regulators to expand their power beyond reasonable bounds, we lose credibility for *all* regulation, even the constructive kind.

Regulation increases the cost of products regulated. A study by Thomas Hopkins of the Rochester Institute of Technology shows that "in 1995 federal regulation cost the American household $7,000 a year (more than the average income tax bill, which was $6,000 per household last year.)" *The Economist* goes on to report:

> Multiple levels of authority produce endless reels of red tape, from the state, county and city governments to semi-autonomous local agencies charged with controlling pollution and other evils. All produce rules which overlap, replicate, and, on occasion, contradict one another.[8]

The government is a monopoly. Though we can vote it out of office, we cannot choose among its products. The government can (and does) change its mind yearly, giving us different conditions of health care, social security, and other goods, changing regulations constantly according to political, not necessarily economic, signals. I would not say, in blanket form, that I trust either government or corporations more. But if I do not trust a corporation, I can buy from another. I cannot do that with government.

Regulation is needed, yet regulation chokes. We do not have the solution. But this little Quakerback is not intended to bring solutions. It is only intended to urge Friends to seek that of truth in minority positions and not to cast their greater trust necessarily in government - or in corporations either - but to think out each situation. Let us use the intelligence that God gave us, as well as our love of people who take positions different from our own.

NOTES

[1] This proposition is first made in my earlier book, *Centuries of Economic Endeavor*, but it is carried over into *The Moral Economy*.

[2] Bovard, James, *Lost Rights: The Destruction of American Liberty,* New York, St. Martin's Press, 1994:153.

[3] Bovard, *op. cit:*202.

[4] Bovard, *op. cit:*35.

[5] *The Moral Economy,* page 152.

[6] "Weird Science at the EPA."

[7] Williams, Stephen F., "Risk Regulation and its Hazards," *Michigan Law Review,* May 1995:1499.

[8] *The Economist,* 7/27/96.

Chapter 19

Touching Hearts and Minds

Can one be both a Quaker and an economist? This question recalls the medieval philosophers, who debated whether the logic of Aristotle coincided with the revelations of God to the prophets. Thomas Aquinas believed that scientific rationalism, while operating within its own laws, nevertheless led to the same conclusions as faith.

The Economist

My economics surrounds my Quakerism, and I have never felt a contradiction. I took my undergraduate degree in economics in 1941, became a Quaker in 1943, and then took my doctorate in economics in 1950. As economist, I was taught that profit is but one side of the coin, the other being service to humankind. Adam Smith - who has been much misunderstood and misquoted - believed that the invisible hand was the hand of God. This I surmise from his less well-known book, *The Theory of Moral Sentiments:* "But by acting according to the dictates of our moral faculties, we necessarily pursue the most effectual means of promoting the happiness of mankind, and thereby may be said, in some sense, to cooperate with the Deity, and to advance as far as in our power the plan of Providence."[1]

Smith assumed an economy of free choice. "Monopoly," he wrote, "is a great enemy to good management, which can never be universally established [except as a result of] that free and universal competition which forces every body to have recourse to [good management for] self-defence."[2] My economics training was based on Adam Smith, but also on other classical and neo-classical economists who constructed the laws of supply and demand.

Their framework was one of cooperation. In a society of individual choice, two persons engage in an economic transaction (buy, sell, hire, or rent) only if both benefit - if not, one of them would not agree. Through the sum of these mutual benefits - in billions of transactions the world over - prosperity is fostered, and human beings achieve the greatest material wealth possible, given existing resources and technology.

In the society of individual choice, human cooperation reaches its highest pinnacle. The suit of clothes that you wear may have come from wool grown in New Zealand, spun into yarn in the Philippines, woven into cloth in China, tailored in Hong Kong, traveled in ships registered in Panama, assembled by wholesalers in England, who shipped it to retailers in the United States. In all of those steps, willing persons bought from and paid each other, because each gained a profit. Yet none of this would have been possible had they not produced a suit of clothing for which the final consumer would pay a price covering all costs. If any charged excessively, the consumer would have purchased elsewhere.

Experimentation, innovation, and invention are innate human qualities. The society of individual choice promotes these qualities, for no monopolist hinders them. As we have seen in previous chapters, monopolies may be private or governmental. The greatest increases in productivity have occurred in those areas (Western societies and Japan) where freedom of choice has historically been practiced.

I have one caveat. A society of individual choice must be one of diffuse power, spread among individuals, associations (such as clubs, unions, interest groups, and political parties), all of which have some power but none so much that one can destroy others to one's monopolistic advantage. In my book, *Centuries of Economic Endeavor,* I have shown how such a society grew, historically, in Japan and northwestern Europe, and in the political descendants of the latter in North America, Australia, and New Zealand.

Imagine the economy as a jig-saw puzzle, solved and sitting on the table. Stretch your imagination, and think of the puzzle as multidimensional (impossible to envision by ordinary eyesight), in which each piece has the potential of rubbing against any other. Each piece is an individual person, and several pieces may voluntarily join to form an interest group, such as a labor union, or a religious committee on national legislation. Each piece or allied group of pieces exerts its power by pushing against the others. If none is so powerful as to subvert others to its interests, it will instead make agreements with other pieces, to mutual advantage. *Decisions are made at the margin.* Classical economics - to which I subscribe - envisions the most desirable world as one where all decisions are made at the margin, between willing individuals, none of which has excessive power over others.

The nineteenth century was the apogee of individual choice in Japan and northwestern Europe. In these two areas, power was more diffuse than it had ever been, and more diffuse than it was anywhere else in the world. These were also the world's most developed areas, that had most conquered hunger, disease, and poverty.

In the twentieth century, Europe, Japan, and the United States all turned toward greater power - presumably "good" power (in government regulations), to overcome "evil" power (in monopolies). Since the Roosevelt administration, many economists have believed it was possible to manage the economy from some central point, such as Washington, D.C. I was one of them. We did not grasp that good power and evil power converge into power alone, and power alone is evil.

Many of my fellow economists - like me - later returned to the original, classical economics. My colleagues who did not, I believe, have been infected by the desire for power - the power to make decisions for others, "in their interests." To me, this power demeans the poor, who are as capable as you and I to make decisions over education, social security, health care, and other benefits. Many of them need financial help, as well as advice and training, and in earlier chapters I have offered a dignified way of providing these.

Toward the end of the twentieth century, however, the "good" power had become overly possessive, overly conscientious, and overly arrogant, so it began suppressing the society of individual choice. This movement has been perceived in the West, and corrective action (deregulation) is being taken. But the process will be slow - again lasting for centuries. Vested interests in regulation will be difficult to dislodge.

The Quaker

To the economist, the other side of profit is human satisfaction. To the Quaker, it is love. Among early Friends - in the seventeenth century - were many business people, whose scrupulousness, honesty, and quality of product are legendary. They earned profit with love. The loving care of the artisan in perfecting handiwork spread into the loving care of the manufacturer and of the merchant. Today, it must apply to the manufacture of every object, such as an airplane, which must be beyond fault, or lives will be lost. It must spread into the service industries, which must always serve the customer well. Not always is this love achieved, not always is it even understood, and airplanes do crash. However, the person whose profit is based on greed - and there are many - will ultimately have 'one's' comeuppance in the world of individual choice, for customers will avoid the products of such a person.

Quakers have always stood for self-reliance, individual initiative, and voluntary cooperation. Just as we do not force our opinions on others in business meetings, so also should we not force them on the world at large, through a uniform plan of health care or social security system to which all must subscribe. We must not force our opinions on others through minimum wages or price controls. In earlier chapters, we have seen that all these social benefits may be obtained through the voluntary cooperation of buyers, sellers, insurers, and others, while governments that offer them ultimately fail to supply them adequately because the people always demand more from the government than they are willing to pay for in taxes.

One exception: a safety net must be spread under the poor. In so doing, we must respect the poor, so that they are empowered to make choices like the rest of us. Therefore, the safety net ideally should be woven out of cash, which the poor may spend as they freely will - just like the rest of us. Sadly, there must be an exception to the exception. If the recipient of public largesse is not trusted to spend it wisely - for example, 'one' would buy drugs and liquor instead of housing and food for 'one's' family - then the safety net may be woven out of vouchers, to be spent on only those designated commodities.

The environment - pure air, pure water, and unsullied fields - must not belong to one monopoly, such as a government that responds to the relative power of short-sighted industries over environmentalists. Instead, the environment should be the province of many nongovernment organizations, each one bound by its charter to respect the bounties of the Lord that have been entrusted to it. Controls must be established through outside monitors.

Respect for the choices of individuals, both poor and not-so-poor, social benefits bought in the private market but subsidized for the poor, asset redistributions from time to time to prevent gross inequalities, help for those who have become lost along the way, and mutual cooperation freely decided upon, all of these show love. Where the economist would say decisions are made at the margin, the Quaker would say there is that of God in every person. Each means the same. We seek truth together.

Aristotle, St. Thomas, Economists, and Quakers

Just as the theologians of the middle ages sought truth both through divine revelation and scientific inquiry - which over centuries were discovered to lead to the same end - so also do the world of economists and the world of Quakers lead ultimately to the same truth, not by law and lawsuit but by touching the hearts and minds of people.

NOTES

[1] Smith, Adam, *The Theory of Moral Sentiments,* 1759 (reprint, Oxford 1979):166.
[2] Smith, Adam, *The Wealth of Nations,* 1776 (reprint, Oxford 1976): 163-4.

Chapter 20

Spiritual Reform

In the Quaker business meeting . . .

> Matters before the Meeting are discussed in a spirit of submission to the Divine ordering until unity is reached. Theoretically there is no coercing of a minority by a majority. . . The final result is in general not a compromise. Often it is a new and unexpected result brought about by the synthesis of different points of view. (Howard Brinton, "Friends for Seventy-Five Years.")

> We must relinquish the desire to own other people, to have power over them, and to force our views on them. (Aotearoa/New Zealand Yearly Meeting, 1987, quoted in Philadelphia Yearly Meeting, *Faith and Practice,* 1997, p. 154.)

Surely it is not possible to apply the spirit of these quotations in the wider world, though Friends might live up to it in our business meetings. Surely one would not expect that city zoning, educational standards, health care, and building codes could be decided upon as "an unexpected result brought about by the synthesis of different points of view." Do not affirmative action, minimum wages, unemployment insurance, and health care for everyone require that the government have power over those who disagree? If the world were to function along Quaker principles, nothing would happen.

Or would it? Quaker practice may be stated emphatically, but it does not lie at an extreme. Rather, Quakers behave along a continuum, with "power over others" at one end and "Sense of the Meeting" at the other. I believe that our current behavior in the wider world is not as close to "Sense-of-the-Meeting" as it might be. Often our organizations propose laws, in matters of work conditions, environmental protection, and racial and gender bias, with love in their hearts but without - I believe - adequately examining why others oppose these laws. Instead, let us touch the hearts and minds of others – seeking that of God in them – to bring about behavior that will benefit us all.

How can we come closer to the Sense-of-the-Meeting end of the continuum? Maybe history can help us.

Medieval European cities would sometimes block the roads to rival cities, so that transient merchants would trade with "us" and not with "them." Sometimes they would silt rival harbors, so ships could not land there. We do not do these things today. What made us change? Because we passed laws against them? Well, we did pass laws, but after studying the history of land tenure and writing two books on it,[1] I have come to believe that laws were not the cause. The cause was that the hearts and minds of people were changed. Consciences came to hold that these practices were not right. How did *that* come about?

For the most part, I believe it happened because of mutual benefit. Historical records show that city fathers agreed with neighboring cities not to block the roads, provided neighbors would do the same. Likewise for silted harbors. Then, to prevent "free riders" (those who would gain by breaking the agreement), laws were passed and enforced. In general, therefore, the laws come *after* hearts and minds are touched. When we pass a law expecting that it will create new consciences, in a few cases we might be right – but more often, I believe, we are wrong. Law without consensus creates hidden resentments that interfere with the smooth functioning of a society.

Historic reform does not come at once. It might seem that slavery in the United States was ended in a single day, with the emancipation proclamation. However, Aristotle's philosophy that holding slaves was virtuous became converted into sinful only after at least twenty centuries, and in some parts of the world slavery is still practiced. Other historic reforms include the abolition of child labor, the end of whipping in the public schools, the conversion of warfare from territorial into ideological, and the end of discrimination according to ethnic origin or gender. The last two have not been completed even today. Where these reforms have been adopted, the benefit has always been mutual – those who disagreed at first began to adopt the reform behavior as time went on, and lo! The reforms had come.

Reforms come on three levels. Spiritually, the lowest is compromise: you give a little, I give a little. The next higher level is consensus, which means "of one mind." Parties in disagreement shed their extremities to adopt a single position that may not have been theirs to begin with. As a Quaker, I believe the highest spiritual level is Sense of the Meeting, which embodies Howard Brinton's philosophy cited in the first paragraph of this chapter: "a new and unexpected result brought about by the synthesis of different points of view." To paraphrase a beloved Quaker saying: "There is no way to get to the Sense of the Meeting. The Sense of the Meeting is the way."

It may seem that the Allied victory in World War II brought about a fourth kind of reform: by power. The changes were dictated by the winning armies. But the Allied powers could not rule Germany and Japan for very long. Because reform by power is impossible, it is not a fourth level.

In today's politics, the most frequent reform is the least spiritual: compromise. The end of the Soviet Union, peace agreements after many wars, health care for every one, and affirmative action are all compromises, to the extent that they have been achieved at all. Yet the art of compromise - rather than stonewalling - should not be denigrated. It is a first historical step toward learning the higher ways of reform.

Friends often confuse "consensus" with "Sense of the Meeting." It has been particularly painful for me to hear Friends use these terms interchangeably, or alternatively to drop "Sense of the Meeting" from their vocabulary and use only "consensus." In the business meetings I have attended, consensus has often been achieved, but true Sense of the Meeting rarely. It remains, however, one of the highest principles of the Society of Friends, one for which we must constantly aim.

It has also been painful for me to hear Friends propose reform that may not take into account the truth found in minority positions. Minimum wages, affirmative action, and sanctions against countries whose governments do not agree with our principles, are all attempts at reform that ignores the minority truth. While such reforms may sometimes win the hearts and minds of that minority after they have occurred, I believe that more often they create resentments, divide a society, and postpone real reform even further.

Historians have long discussed whether culture change leads the law, or the law leads culture change. Sometimes one leads, sometimes the other. After reading world history for a period of thirty years and writing my major lifetime opus on it,[2] I have come to believe that more often than not, culture change leads the law. Therefore, true reform requires touching the hearts and minds of people. Sometimes after that, a law is necessary.

In the limited time that I spent with each Friends' gathering, I did not adequately express my hopes for spiritual reform. I believe they were not always understood, and I may not have understood the positions of those who disagreed with me. The purpose of this book has been to clarify and expand on my own expressions, in hopes that Friends will somehow take the dialogue further, as the Way opens.

NOTES

[1] Powelson, John P., *The Story of Land,* Cambridge MA, Lincoln Institute of Land Policy, 1988, and
Powelson, John P., and Stock, Richard, *The Peasant Betrayed,* revised edition, Washington DC, Cato Institute, 1990.
[2] *Centuries of Economic Endeavor.*

Chapter 21

Seeking Truth Together

by Jane Kashnig

Nearly three decades ago, I had three experiences which, considered together, convinced me I am Quaker. The first was the experience of Meeting for Worship. The second experience happened in a business meeting. I was a new attender unfamiliar with Friends' practices. A matter was being decided. Some spoke passionately about a particular course of action. Those who held different views were equally passionate. Then I spoke. "Why don't we just vote on that?" There was a moment of stunned silence, and I was bewildered by the shocked looks of others. The clerk, Chuck Wright, spoke next. "Friend Jane has just pointed out that we are being argumentative and persuasive in our speech." (Is that what I did? I thought.) "Let us settle into silence and seek the truth in this matter together."

We all know what "argumentative" means. By "persuasive," Chuck referred to charismatic crowd movers who do not use their eloquence in the service of truth. Ultimately they do not persuade, because only the truth persuades.

The silence that followed felt just the way worship had felt to me. After a length of time, someone spoke of a third way, previously unconsidered and totally different from the two views that had been espoused. Another Friend said a special phrase I'd never heard before, "I unite with that." Heads nodded. "That Friend speaks my mind," a third said. The clerk spoke "the sense of the meeting," and silent worship followed without any call for silence. At the time, I knew I'd been part of something precious and special. It seemed like a miracle. Later I learned the name for it, a gathered meeting. Over the decades that have followed, I've learned something else as well - a gathered meeting for business is rare even though my heart tells me it does not have to be.

What I now notice is that truth seeking together is work. "And then a miracle happened" does not describe what occurs even when the outcome may seem miraculous and we may feel blessed by divine presence.

I always notice an extraordinary willingness to sift through statements searching for bits of truth like beachcombers seeking rare shells amid the vastness of the sands. These finds are culled out and together we turn this and that bit of truth over and over making the decision to put it in our collection or return it to the sea. An idea does not have to be fully formed or even "on target." If there is a lot of "sand" in a presentation, there is trust that there must be a shell in there somewhere. (I do admit it takes extraordinary gifts to recognize argumentative and persuasive speech from a call for a vote. But how much more effective this was for us all in our understanding of the process than just telling me that Quakers don't vote!) This kind of listening is not a ploy to make another feel understood or to lead a person on so that they may then be persuaded by different arguments. It is listening in order to be informed and transformed by hearing the truth of another.

I also notice speech becomes more precise with less hyperbole, shorter in length, more direct, with little repetition. Facts are differentiated from opinions, thoughts, or feelings. If a "fact" is stated, the careful speaker frequently notes the basis of this "fact" so others may assess the nature of this "truth" for themselves. When the speaker cites direct personal experience as the basis of truth, Friends have a way of affirming the person and the experience without assuming the experience is universal. Argumentative and persuasive speech, I found, are frowned upon because they are seen as ways to shift opinions, not as ways to seek truth.

Amid all of this is the certainty that seeking truth together is holy work. Silence happens or sometimes may be called for, not as a device to halt a speaker or subdue emotions but so the divine participant may be heard more clearly. Time becomes irrelevant. Other forms that our worship takes, and our fellowship, both nurture and are nurtured by this process.

I'm really not sure why gathered business meetings are so rare. But I have observed some behaviors in myself and others that I think are clues. Many in our meetings either stand aside from those who passionately hold different views from their own or they push these people to the margins of the meeting community. Speaking of myself, I notice I tend to seek fellowship with those who more-or-less share my worldview; and if the only worldview I share with another is our opinions of the weather and the seasons, our conversations are short and eventually infrequent. Attending business meeting can be painful for someone who is frequently called to say, "Friends, I am not comfortable with this." Nonattendance is often the only comfortable alternative. I hesitate to use a word as strong as "shunning" to describe behaviors I see in my beloved community. Nevertheless, we have ways of making it clear which ideas are "correct" without ever requiring adherence to a creed.

This fills me with sorrow. I mourn the loss of sincere seekers, good people in our midst who are no longer actively involved with us because they are aligned with the "wrong" political party or have an "incorrect" view of cosmology or God - or whatever has led to the sense of being an outsider. I miss the richness, vibrancy, and the piercing light of passions, the fervor of personally meaningful words - all replaced by Quaker grays that make us all sound the same. I see people whom I would love to share religious community with who are put off not by our way of worship but by our apparent inability to explore difficult, meaningful issues as a religious community. I know this because they attend worship regularly until their first business meeting. Then they say something like, this is not for me.

When Jack Powelson asked me for help in getting clear about his calling to write this book for Friends, my rejoinder was to ask whether he might consider writing on a less difficult and divisive topic, such as war and peace. This comment was made half in jest, but it also reflects direct experience. As a meeting treasurer, then convener of the finance committee, member of the building committee, and with long involvements with budgets and fund raising with Quakers, I have never seen the topics of money, finance, or economics addressed "in the manner of Friends." The best I have seen is compromise, although most often I see conflict avoidance. In contrast, I've frequently seen meetings address issues of war and peace in a concerned, consistent manner. However, there remains something within me that cannot accept the premise that the Quaker way works for all things except those involving money. This is especially a concern for me because I believe economic issues are among the roots of war and resolving these issues will build a foundation for peace.

So when Jack became certain that he should proceed in this writing and expressed his intent to speak his concerns in the manner of Friends, I was supportive. Now I encourage us all to look for the "shells" in Jack's sand, however many or few you personally find. For those who are impressed with the number of shells you find in these writings, I hope you notice Jack's careful listening and attention to the concerns of others who feel differently. It is also my hope that those who find Jack's views are mostly sand will still recognize a few shells, in the idea that a society of increased individual choice and responsibility is consistent with Friends' values. Please consider whether, as Jack proposes, such a society may truly help the poor more than government intervention on their behalf. Then the way will be open to searching for truth together - no matter what the political party or the label. And if you find shells and sand, and that may be all of us, try doing both. It is my sincerest hope that when we abandon argumentative and persuasive speech, listen to each other's truths, speak carefully our own truths, and above all, listen to the voice of the divine participant, a third way will emerge that we can unite with.

Appendix on the World Trade Organization

After *Seeking Truth Together* had been sent to the printer, and it was too late to make changes except in this Appendix, Protestor and Advocate decided upon a reunion to talk about events since Chapter 14 had been written.

P: Did you see *Friends Journal* of March 2000, with its anti-WTO emphasis?

A: Yes, it was extremely one-sided, and if it represents Friends' thinking, they have a long way to go before they seek truth together with those who disagree. The monster bearing the sign "WTO - Corporate Greed" does not attract me toward Quakers as Seekers of the Truth. They seem to think they have found it.

P: What do you mean?

A: They take just one side on a big issue where honest people disagree. The big disagreement is whether regulations that discriminate against trade are intended to protect local industry or to protect the environment. For example, the German beer industry had standards of purity far higher than any other country. Clearly they were designed to keep foreign beer out of Germany, not to protect the environment. The European Court of Justice decided against them. University Meeting in Seattle declares, "We are especially concerned that the WTO has already caused several countries around the world to overturn important environmental and public health laws." Has University Meeting studied those laws to determine that they were not intended instead as protection of local producers? Why do all the Quakers just assume that the environment is being abused when these anti-trade laws might be for protection instead? There was not a whit of evidence in the *Friends Journal* that any Quaker had studied these laws.

P: But how can you tell the difference between environment-protection laws and those protecting domestic producers? The author mentioned that "efforts to protect endangered sea turtles from fishing nets constituted an unfair 'restraint of trade.'" Our law (that shrimp nets should be designed to exclude sea turtles) was clearly planned to save the turtles, and when we exclude shrimp from other

114

countries that do not have these laws, that is not to protect our fishers of shrimp.

A: Of course. It was similar to the tuna-dolphin debate. And likewise, the WTO had no power to order the United States to change the law. All it did was to say that the United States could not forbid the import of shrimp (mainly from Southeast Asia) because of that law. Does the United States have the right to deny markets to Asian shrimpers because they do not live up to our standards? If it does do so, shrimp-producing countries may retaliate against U.S. exports. I don't understand why Quakers - known as great conciliators - do not bring out all sides in articles such as these, so that we may be aware of how much our environmental standards reduce the standard of living of poor people, such as Asian shrimpers and Mexican tuna-fishers.

P: What about genetically-modified organisms? The Europeans ban the import of genetically-modified beef from the United States because they fear it may cause cancer; the United States objected; and the WTO found in favor of the United States.

A: That was because the Europeans had not conducted scientific studies that determined that harm comes from genetically-modified beef. Americans eat it all the time, and there is no evidence of danger. Furthermore, the Europeans have not lifted the ban, and the matter is still under negotiation.

But in Montreal in January 2000, the WTO agreed on the Biosafety Protocol. This provides that while the matter is still under study, the Europeans may temporarily continue the ban.[1]

P: But I agree with *Friends Journal* that the WTO promotes corporate greed.

A: On the contrary, here is a ruling that will definitely be costly to corporations. At present, many U.S. corporations export, not to the final customer, but to some subsidiary in the Virgin Islands or Guam or elsewhere that is partially exempt from U.S. profits taxes on certain goods. The subsidiary sells these goods to the foreign buyer and remits the profit to the U.S. parent company without paying the tax. This is all legal under the Foreign Sales Corporation Plan. In February 2000 the WTO ruled that this practice constitutes unfair subsidization.[2] This ruling will cost billions of dollars to about 6,000 multinational corporations, including Microsoft, Ford Motor Company, and Exxon Mobil. Before reaching a conclusion on the WTO and corporate greed, don't you think Quakers should take into account WTO rulings that remove privileges from multinational corporations?

P: Friends Journal pointed out that the police were responsible for the violence in Seattle, whereas all but a few protestors were nonviolent. The nonviolent protestors even tried to restrain the violent ones.

A: Forty-seven years ago JP (the author of this book) wrote in *Friends Intelligencer* (the precursor to *Friends Journal*) that "though nonviolent resistance may be a doctrine of love, it is nevertheless a weapon of coercion and as such may be used in an immoral as well as a moral way."[3] His article, "Nonviolence and Understanding," appealed for "positive approaches to mutual agreement rather than the means of resolving a conflict in a predetermined way."

Let us consider the viewpoint of the police. Their job includes keeping streets open so that anyone may use 'one's' right of passage. The protestors were denying the rights of WTO delegates to enter the conference building. They did so nonviolently, but they were still denying rights to innocent people. The police, frustrated and vastly outnumbered, resorted to tear gas and rubber bullets and brought in helmeted riot police and National Guard units. They threw no bombs and shot no rifles. Were they violent?

[The recording clerk noted that the sides were still far apart, but she could see some consistencies in each position. To P, the environment was the main concern. P was willing to believe that any law calling itself environmental was indeed environmental, and that it was not intended to protect a favorite producer. A, on the other hand, was far more concerned for promoting international trade. He believed that the WTO rulings against "environmental" laws had really been made to knock down laws protecting local producers against foreigners, and often associated with the environment in only a minimal way. He was also concerned for less developed countries and their ability to raise themselves out of poverty by exporting.

(JP, an economic historian, assured him that all more developed countries today, including the United States, had built their prosperity initially on international trade and investment.) A had also consulted trade economists on these laws, and he thought P and his friends reached decisions without adequate knowledge. P, on the other hand, associated international trade with profits and greed. A believed more in the economic role of profits which was brought out Chapter 15. He considered P to be a "corporationist," as defined in Chapter 17, though of course he was too polite to say so.

JP was asked whether he stood by his statement of forty-seven years ago. Yes, he said, except that instead of nonviolence as a means to immoral as well as moral ends, he would now say it could be used to deny the legitimate rights of others, as was the case in Seattle.

P and A agreed to meet again in a year, to discuss what had happened in the meantime. They departed after a moment of silence.]

NOTES

[1] *The Economist,* 2/5/00.
[2] *New York Times* and *Wall Street Journal,* 2/24/00.
[3] Third Month 28, 1953.

Other Books by Jack Powelson

The Moral Economy, Ann Arbor, University of Michigan Press, 1998.

Centuries of Economic Endeavor: Parallel Paths in Japan and Europe and their Contrast with the Third World, Ann Arbor, University of Michigan Press, 1994.

The Peasant Betrayed: Agriculture and Land Reform in the Third World, with Richard Stock, revised edition by Cato Institute, Washington, D.C., 1990; original edition: Cambridge, Massachusetts, Lincoln Institue of Land Policy, 1987.

The Story of Land: A World History of Land Tenure and Agrarian Reform, Cambridge, Massachusetts, Lincoln Institute of Land Policy, 1988.

Dialogue with Friends, Quakerback, Boulder, Colorado, Horizon Society Publications, 1988.

Facing Social Revolution: The Personal Journey of a Quaker Economist, Quakerback, Boulder, CO, Horizon Society Publications, 1987.

Threat to Development: Pitfalls of the New International Economic Order, with William Loehr, Boulder, CO, Westview Press, 1983.

The Economics of Development and Distribution, with William Loehr, New York, Harcourt, Brace, Jovanovich, 1981.

A Select Bibliography on Economic Development, with Annotations, Boulder, CO, Westview Press, 1979.

Income Distribution, Poverty, and Economic Development, Co-editor, with William Loehr, Boulder, CO, Westview Press, 1977.

Development Plan, 1974/78, Government of Kenya, Nairobi, Kenya, Government Printing Office, Co-author (government publication, not attributed), 1974.

Employment in Africa, Co-editor (with Philip Ndegwa), Geneva, International Labor Office, 1973.

Institutions of Economic Growth: A Theory of Conflict Management in Developing Countries, Princeton, N.J., Princeton University Press, 1972.

Latin America: Today's Economic and Social Revolution, New York, McGraw-Hill, 1964, with editions in Spanish and Portuguese.

National Income and Flow of Funds Analysis, New York, McGraw-Hill, 1960, with edition in Spanish by Fondo de Cultura Económica, Mexico

Economic Accounting, New York, McGraw-Hill, 1955, with edition in Spanish by Fondo de Cultura Económica, Mexico.

NOTE: The Quakerbacks carry author's name as "Jack Powelson." All others carry "John P. Powelson."

Articles in Quaker Journals by Jack Powelson

"Emweakenment and The Moral Economy," *Quaker Life,* March 1999 and *Friends Journal,* December 1998.

"World Without Borders," *Friends Bulletin,* December 1998.

"The Brown Cushion," *Friends Journal,* May 1993.

"Seeking the Truth," *Friends Journal,* August 1991.

"Civil Disobedience: When Do I Break the Law?" in *Friends Journal,* May 1989.

"Sanctuary," *Friends Bulletin,* May 1985.

"The Soviet Union, South Africa, and Us" (with Kenneth B. Powelson), *Friends Journal,* November 1, 1984.

"How to Achieve Social Justice with Peace and No Champions" *Right Sharing News,* Friends World Committee for Consultation, Philadelphia PA, vol. XI, no. 1, January/February 1984.

"Military Spending and the Economy," *Friends Bulletin,* vol. 52, no. 5, January 1984.

Holistic Economics and Social Protest, Pendle Hill Pamphlet no. 252, Pendle Hill, Wallingford, PA, 1983.

"El Salvador and Quaker Credibility," *Friends Journal,* pp. 7-10, August 1-15, 1981.

"Friends' Affluence and the Third World," *Friends Journal,* pp. 11-13, March 15, 1981.

"Feeling Comfortable," *Friends Journal,* p. 17, May 15, 1980.

"Manuel and Tom," *Friends Bulletin,* pp. 88-89, April 1977.

"Values and Membership," *Friends Bulletin,* pp. 71-72, March 1977.

"When Would I Kill?," *Friends Bulletin,* pp. 21-22, Oct. 1976.

"The Decline of Commitment," *Friends Bulletin,* pp.105-106, May 1976.

"China, Freedom, and Friends," *Friends Bulletin,* March, 1976, pp. 88-89.

"Friends and Crises of Conscience," *Friends Journal,* pp. 107-108. February 15, 1976.

"The Inverse Arrogance of Friends," *Friends Bulletin,* September, 1975, with continuation in October, 1975.

"They Saw and Were Broadened," *Friends Journal,* June 15, 1966.

"Nonviolence and Understanding," *Friends Intelligencer,* March 28, 1953.

"A Boatload of Students," *Friends Intelligencer,* November 29, 1947.

"Why Fear Failure When the Dice are Loaded?" *Young Friends Correspondent* (New York), October 1944.

"Falsehood: The Real Atrocity," *Young Friends Correspondent* (New York), June 1944.

"Inventory," *Young Friends Correspondent* (New York), April 1944.

"The Nature of the Enemy," *Young Friends Correspondent* (New York), February 1944.

"Let's Get This War Bond Situation Straight," *Young Friends Correspondent* (New York), December 1943.

"Wherein Lies the Fervor of the Friends?" *Young Friends Correspondent* (New York), October 1943.

NOTE: All Quaker articles carry the name "Jack Powelson." Articles in academic/scholarly journals (not listed here) carry the name "John P. Powelson."